I0815462

MONA
PAST
AND
PRESENT

The Mona Chapel

MONA PAST AND PRESENT

The History and Heritage of the Mona Campus, University of the West Indies

SUZANNE FRANCIS BROWN

University of the West Indies Press
Jamaica • Barbados • Trinidad & Tobago

Department of History and Archaeology
University of the West Indies, Mona, Jamaica

The University of the West Indies Press
1A Aqueduct Flats
Kingston 7 Jamaica WI
www.uwipress.com

ISBN 976-640-158-6 (cloth)
ISBN 976-640-159-4 (paper)

 Published 2004

A catalogue record of this book is available
from the National Library of Jamaica.

Photographs of the University of the West Indies: Suzanne Francis Brown, Jeremy Francis, Ruth Wilson and Robert Harris. Other photographs and illustrations by courtesy of the National Library of Jamaica, the Government of Jamaica Archives, the UWI Mona campus Main Library's West Indies Collection, the UWI Archive and Records Management Programme, the UK Foreign and Commonwealth Office, the University of Glasgow Archive, the Catholic Chancery, and the UWI Public Relations Office. Stereographs on pp. 10–11 reproduced from the collection of the Library of Congress. Tables and annotated maps by Suzanne Francis Brown.

Cover photo by J. Tyndale-Biscoe
Cover and book design by Robert Harris
E-mail: roberth@cwjamaica.com
Set in Garamond 11/13.5 x 18
Printed and bound in Canada.

"The Mona Campus is unique in the Kingston/St Andrew area in the range of historic landscapes that it contains. The most notable of the features are the sites of the two sugar works belonging to the Mona and Papine Estates, with the associated extensive sections of aqueduct dating from 1758, the botanical indicators of slave and free plantation workers' settlements, the buildings surviving from the Gibraltar Camp of World War II, and the still developing structures of the university itself. All of these features can be interpreted within the broader context of the natural landscape and changing land use patterns of the area, providing an important educational opportunity as well as the basis for a physically attractive campus."

"Report to the Principal of the ad hoc Committee on the Preservation and Development of the Historic Features of the Mona Campus", April 23, 1992

"There is a narrow valley in Jamaica behind the mountain nearly 2,000 feet high, covered with bushes, light acacias and dogwood . . . In the centre of the valley are the ruins of a great sugar estate, the mill, an aqueduct . . . besides huts built in the war for refugees from Gibraltar."

Script, BBC Overseas Service programme introduced by Henry Swanzy and broadcast June 9, 1952, titled "University College of the West Indies"

CONTENTS

FOREWORD

The Mona campus of the University of the West Indies – the first to be established, and indeed the *only* campus for a decade after the foundation of the University College of the West Indies in 1948 – sits on a site of remarkable historical, cultural and architectural diversity. Although this has long been recognized, details of this rich diversity have hitherto remained relatively inaccessible to the curious observer and to the general public. Guides to the campus do exist, but they are hard to come by and tend to deal only with specific periods and themes. The present publication represents the first attempt to pull together the various strands and layers of the historical past of the campus into a coherent whole.

The area constituting the Mona campus has been home to an eclectic range of peoples who have left their mark, to a greater or lesser extent, on the history of Jamaica and on the campus topography. Today, of course, it is the architecture of the late-twentieth-century University that dominates but does not wholly obscure relics of the more distant past – the eighteenth-century aqueduct, for example, or the bookkeeper's cottage of the old Mona Estate (home, since 2000, to the department's Archaeology Laboratory), or the wooden buildings of the Gibraltar Camp period.

The burgeoning construction of the past ten years – an impressive reflection of the dynamism and vitality of the modern University – has radically transformed the aspect of the campus. It seemed most appropriate, in the middle of this period of most rapid change, to stand back and take stock, and to undertake a comprehensive inventory and record of the history and heritage of the campus.

The Department of History and its staff have accumulated a good deal of experience in this domain, through the organization of tours, archaeological excavations and in the drafting of the 1992 Report to the Principal on the historic features of the campus. Yet when it came to considering who might write this publication, the decision was a gratifyingly easy one to make. Suzanne Francis Brown, a graduate of the master's programme in Heritage Studies and an experienced journalist and author in her own right, had just completed an excellent research paper: "Heritage and Development at the UWI Mona Campus". Happily for the department, she was agreeable to our proposal, and has produced a fascinating compendium of text and illustrations, which does full justice to the richness of the campus past. We are most grateful to the Campus Principal, Professor Kenneth Hall, for seeing the merit in this project, and for providing the funds which have enabled us to carry it through to fruition.

Jonathan Dalby
Department of History and Archaeology

ACKNOWLEDGEMENTS

My thanks to the Department of History and Archaeology of the University of the West Indies, Mona campus for the opportunity to pursue research explored during the preparation of a 2001 MA Heritage Studies paper, "Heritage and Development at the UWI Mona Campus"; and to Professor Kenneth Hall and the Office of the Principal at UWI Mona for supporting the initiative. The Editorial Committee comprised former Head of History Dr Jonathan Dalby, Public Relations Manager Mrs Carroll Edwards, Mr Francis Felix of the Business Development Office, and Professor Patrick Bryan, Dr Veront Satchell and Mrs Jenny Jemmott of the History Department.

Thanks are also due to many persons, within and outside of the History Department, who generously contributed references, ideas, suggestions or names of persons who should be pursued for information. Special mention is made of Professor Barry Higman, who provided records he had collected and acted as a reader for the publication. The staffs of the UWI Main Library's West Indies Collection, the UWI Archives and Record Management Programme, the UWI Public Relations Office, and the National Library of Jamaica were unfailingly helpful. Mr Leonard Notice of UWI's Department of Geography and Geology and Peter Francis and Associates assisted with the maps.

Aside from formal texts and manuscripts, interviews or conversations with the following persons during 2001 and early 2002 provided invaluable information: Mr Allan Rae, son of Gibraltar Camp Commandant Ernest Rae; Dr Owen Minott, member of the first class, University College of the West Indies (UCWI); Mr Cedric Harper, UCWI student, Irvine Hall Warden, later Dean of Students; and Mr Allan Kirton, UCWI student, whose memories of campus life helped clarify areas muddied by time; Mr Karl "Jerry" Craig, artist, educator, Chairman of the UWI Mona Landscape Committee in 2001, whose father Major Karl Craig, was the UCWI's first Steward; and Mr Uwe Zitzow, who was interned as a child, with his parents, at the Mona Family Camp.

In addition, Mr Tony Gambrill, who presently occupies the Mona Great House, helpfully shared his own investigations into the provenance of the house, including a 1990 Jamaica National Heritage Trust report on old foundations beneath the present floorboards. Professors David Buisseret and Kofi Agorsah shared information, in some instances via e-mail, related to their respective periods at Mona.

Support from friends and family smoothed the process of research and writing – with special thanks to Professor Aggrey Brown, himself a veteran UWI academic and administrator, who was a willing listener and reader.

Aerial view of the Mona campus environs, 2002

THE UWI MONA CAMPUS

Since 1948, the Mona campus of the University of the West Indies (UWI) has occupied a square mile of land in the parish of St Andrew, on the outskirts of the city of Kingston, in the island of Jamaica.

Before that, during World War II, some of the land was the site of Gibraltar Camp, a village of barracks occupied by some 1,500 evacuated Gibraltarians; as well as an assortment of European refugees from Hitler's Blitzkrieg – most of them Jews; and interned enemy aliens. Even earlier, from the mid-seventeenth century, the Mona and Papine sugar estates were centred within these boundaries. Remnants of their sugar works, including the stone aqueduct, which brought water from the Hope River to turn the wheels and crush the cane, can still be seen on the campus. African slaves served the English and creole plantation owners, and their descendants worked as free labourers on the estates joined, or sometimes replaced in the late nineteenth century, by East Indian indentured labourers who grew cane and various small crops or raised livestock. The English had replaced the Spanish on the Liguanea Plain in 1655, gradually spreading their control across the island. The Spanish themselves had overborne the Taino or Arawak people who preceded them.

The landscape on which the history of the area has been played out, is one of gently sloping land in a wide valley between the Port Royal, Dallas and Long Mountains. The slope steepens towards the site's south-western boundary which runs up to the 800-foot contour on the Long Mountain. Towards the site's eastern boundary, an escarpment runs generally northeast to southwest, with the campus playing fields on a wide river terrace at the bottom of the slope, some 100 feet (30 metres) above the present bed of the Hope River. This river has provided water, as well as construction materials, to the estates in the area since the mid-seventeenth century.

Undergraduates over the years have remembered their first approach to UWI: through the main gate and up Queen's Way toward the Senate House, with the hills curving protective arms in the distance.

Ruins dot the campus, most of them recalling the sugar and war years. Little or nothing marks the earliest periods. Taino remains have been found in the vicinity, but there is no evidence to confirm whether they actually walked these acres. Similarly, there has been mention of Spanish relics brought in from the hills behind Hope Gardens and near Mount Mansfield, but there are no documents available in Jamaica which record ownership or use of specific tracts of land by the Spanish-Jamaicans. However, these settlers are known to have had extensive ranches or *hatos*, where long-horned cattle ran wild until round-up time. There is a reference, in an unpublished paper titled "Freedom in Jamaica", which dates back to the 1920s, to the whole Liguanea Plain having formed one huge hacienda "belonging to a Spanish lady who lived at Cavalier's Penn". The author, Winifred M. Cousins, notes that the English "ungallantly dispossessed her".

The Spanish-Jamaicans had moved onto the Liguanea Plain in the 1530s, from Jamaica's north coast where they had settled in 1509 – some 15 years after Cristóbal Colón's first visit in 1494. While there are no known land records from that period, there is documentation of the sugar cane and other plants and trees which they introduced. Thera Edwards, in "A Floral History of the Mona Campus", lists:

> Citrus fruits; fig, plantain and banana; pomegranate; ginger; indigo; cocoa; avocado; chocho; grains such as wheat, barley and rice; chick peas; onion and garlic; radish; cabbage and cauliflower; carrot and lettuce; eggplant; gungo/pigeon peas; fruit such as melon and grape; and trees: castor oil, cassia, guango, poinciana, coconut and logwood.

Favourites of the Amerindians were already common. These included field plants such as cassava, sweet potato, yampi, arrowroot, coco, corn and tobacco; garden plants such as ground-nut, pineapple, squash, pepper, beans, callaloo, cucumber, sweet cup and prickly pear; trees and shrubs including sweetsop, soursop, custard apple, guinep, stinking toe, macca fat, plums, cashew, mammee, starapple and guava; as well as annatto, calabash and cotton for domestic purposes.

While many of these trees and plants remain common in the area, the most prominent botanical markers on the Mona campus are groves of ackee trees, popular food sources which were traditionally found near slave villages on local plantations. Their locations confirm the sites of the old Papine and Mona Estate villages, also marked on local survey maps. The campus was also well known for groves of mango trees at one time. Besides the botanical tracers and the old cut-stone, brick and wooden remains, there are historical records in texts, old documents, maps and illustrations, which help to tell the tale of this place from the time when the English took control of Jamaica in the seventeenth century.

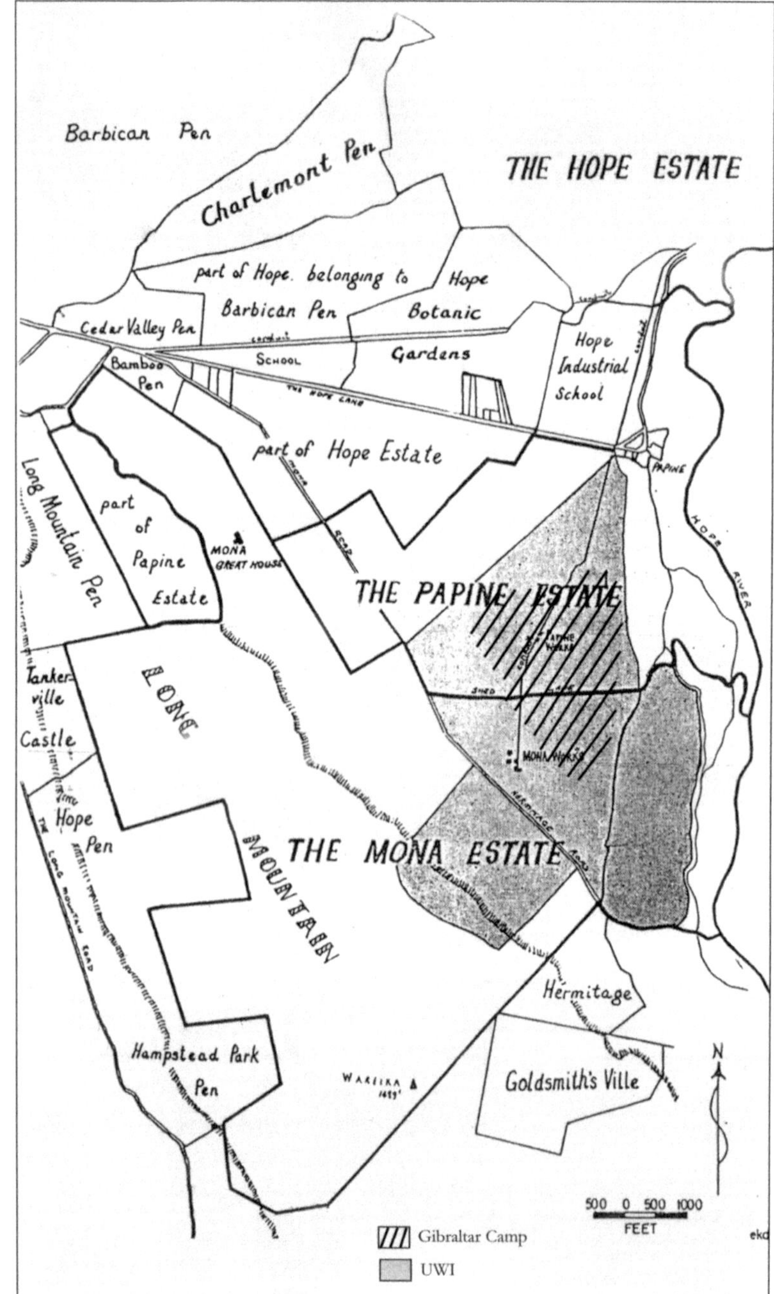

Map to show relationship of Mona and Papine sugar estates, Gibraltar Camp, and the UWI Mona campus (based on a 1965 student pamphlet)

One of the Jamaican stamps that has celebrated the UCWI/UWI over time

WHEN SUGAR WAS KING

English Arrivants

A force of English soldiers, under the command of Admiral William Penn and General Robert Venables, landed at Passage Fort in St Catherine on May 10, 1655, fresh from defeat in Hispaniola. They challenged Jamaica's weak Spanish authorities, and were soon entrenched in the south-east. Colonel William Brayne, and subsequently Colonel Edward D'Oyley, were among the commanders sent out by British Lord Protector Oliver Cromwell to complete the takeover of Jamaica. Among the early military placements were several companies of soldiers on the Liguanea Plain, usually near to the rivers, including the Hope River in the east.

At first, civilian settlement of the area was slow, apparently due in part to recalcitrance on the part of the military men stationed there. By 1662, a report notes that Liguanea had a population of 881 persons, the vast majority of them male and white. A September 1670 survey of the district records 81 land holdings by individual proprietors, nine of them – including Major Richard Hope – having title to some two-thirds of the land up to then distributed. The population of the parish of St Andrew, in which Liguanea falls, was then reported as 1,552 persons comprising 194 families. Three years later, the parish population had nearly doubled, with some half of the number being Negro slaves.

Major Hope, Richard Brayne, Captain William Valette, Thomas William and William Morgan are some of the prominent names associated with land grants and patents west of the Hope River during the period 1664 to 1669. Planters with smaller properties appear to have settled on the fringes of the larger estates, perhaps to take advantage of the large estates' private roads and other facilities.

Edward Long, in his 1774 *History of Jamaica,* volume 2, notes of the Liguanea area:

> One of the Oliverian regiments first settled here, under the command of Colonel Archbould and Major Hope, who, with Sir William Beeston, possessed the best and largest share of this whole tract. Few of the sugar-plantations are remoter from the harbour than six or seven miles; the interior or hilly part being chiefly employed in the cultivation of coffee and provisions. The roads here are in general firm; the sugar of excellent

Population of St Andrew in the Late Seventeenth Century

	Total population		**Families**	**Whites**			**Negroes**
				Men	Women	Children	
Liguanea	1662	881		553	149	125	54
St Andrew	1670	1,552	194				
	1673	2,677		565	274	430	1,408

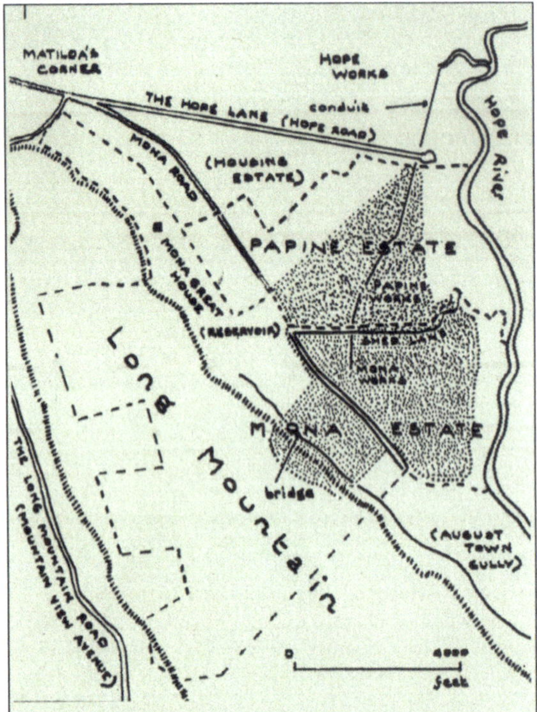

Map showing how the UWI relates to the Mona and Papine estates (University of the West Indies Mona Campus: An Historic Guide)

> quality; and the carriage to and from the town so easy, that the estates are justly esteemed very valuable.

Figures in Long's history indicate that in 1761, there were 9,024 Negroes labouring on 30 sugar estates in St Andrew to produce 2,600 hogsheads of sugar annually.

It is under the English that these and other surviving local records began to be maintained, including those documenting the ownership of estates at Hope, Papine and Mona. The Hope Estate, immediately north of the Papine Estate, dates back to early land awards to Major Richard Hope, and is mentioned here because of its link to the development of the aqueduct, the most outstanding of the historic remnants left on the UWI site.

While Hope Estate was clearly named after its earliest English owner, the genesis of the names Mona and Papine is less certain. It has been suggested that Mona may come from the Roman name for Anglesey or the Isle of Man. The name appears in 1767, during a transfer of the property. Papine, rendered "Papin" on a local 1766 survey map, is also the name of a village in Banffshire, Scotland. There is a story that Alexander Grant, the Scotsman who took charge of the estate in 1756, was at the Mill of Papine in Scotland when he heard that he had inherited property in Jamaica, and he brought the name here in memory of that moment. Local Chancery records for 1797 show that Grant still had estates at Arndilly, Scotland, when he died.

An early boiling and curing house for sugar

Muscovado and Melasses

Mona and Papine were sugar estates, and it is appropriate to quote from Edward Long's 1774 *History of Jamaica*, volume 3, which discusses sugar production at some length, from the viewpoint of an Englishman when sugar was king. Cane juice, Long notes, converted to muscovado, refined sugar, melasses [*sic*] and rum; with the remainder consisting of water, scum and dregs from which rum could also be distilled. A portion of skimmings was given to mules and hogs on most estates.

Long reflects concerns about production and waste:

> Many reckon 200 gallons of rum to 3 hogsheads of sugar, and this may be admitted, where skimmings and melasses are both of them applied: in general, it may be computed, that only about one-fourth part of the ingredients used in the distillation of rum, consists of melasses. In this case, 100 lb. wt. of muscovado is proportioned to 1 gallon of melasses, or 4 gallons of rum; i.e. one puncheon or 112 gallons or 2 hogsheads of 1400 lb. each, nett weight. There is a great waste of this syrup in various ways; in the curing-house, the cisterns, etc and much is left in the sugar hogsheads, undrained. The waste in a hogshead of sugar on the voyage home is very frequently 100 lb. wt., which chiefly (if not entirely) is melasses; from ill-cured sugar the drain is still greater, amounting sometimes to one-third of the whole weight shipped. 100 lb. may, therefore, be called the average per hogshead. This, on 1,000 hogsheads, is 100,000 lb., which probably might have yielded 8,750 puncheons of rum, worth upwards of £12,000 Sterling.

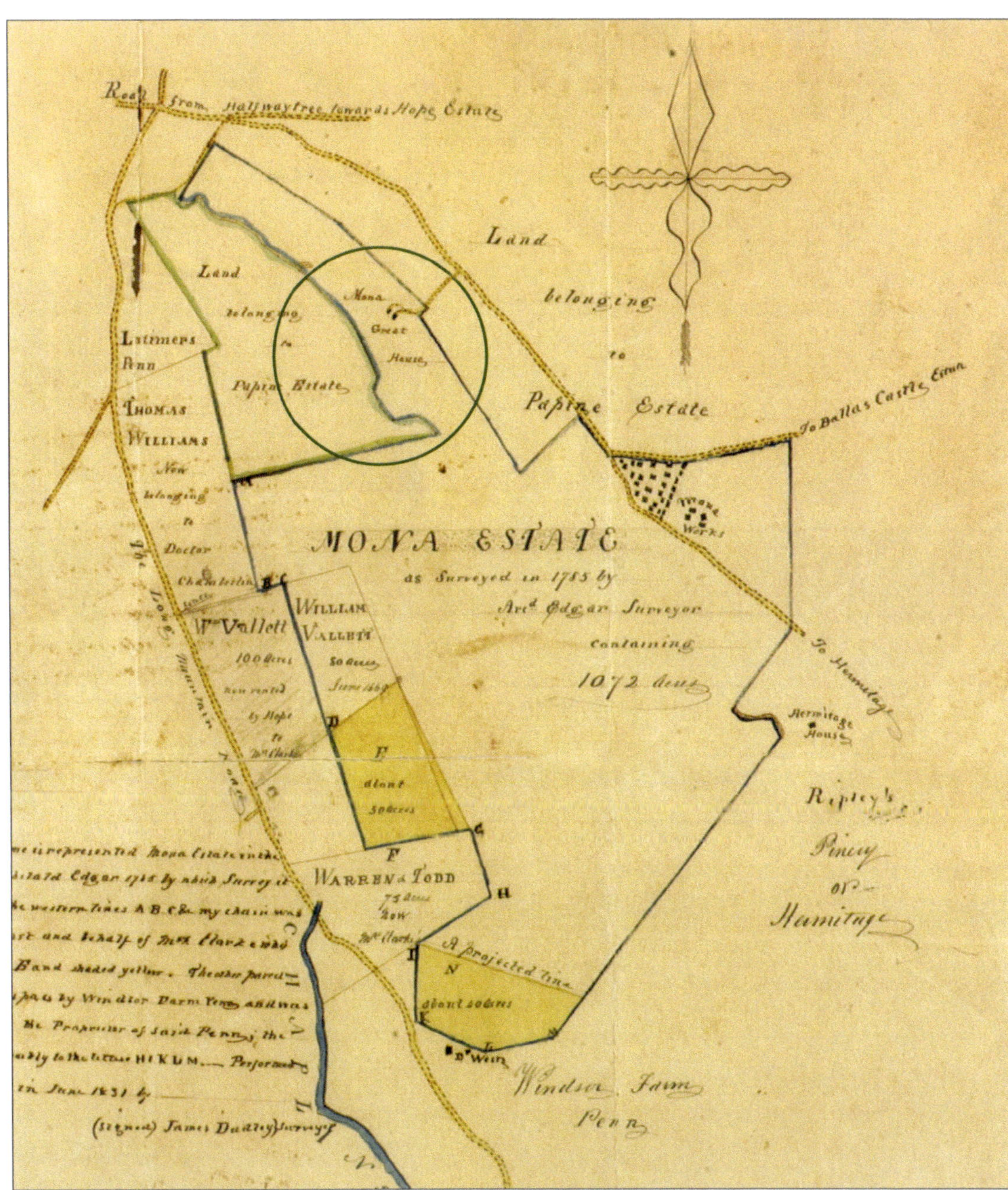

1831 survey map of Mona Estate

Mona Estate

Survey maps and plans can help tell the story of estates such as Mona and Papine. The location of the Mona Great House provides an example. There have been tales of a site somewhere inside the present College Common area, within the bounds of the UWI. Yet there is also a Mona Great House located on a hillside overlooking the Mona Road, within the bounds of the original sugar estate but outside of the UWI campus. It is an old, but clearly not an ancient, house. How to resolve the disparity?

A November 10, 1804 map by Murdock and Keeffe, Surveyors, represents "the figure of several parcels of land in the parish of St Andrew laid down from actual traverses in order to show the situation and extent of Mona Plantation". The map, in the National Library of Jamaica collection, is damaged in an area apparently between the August Town Gully and the Hope River, which covers most of the portion of Mona now part of the UWI property. However, two sections within this area, still legible, are marked, respectively, "Brayne belonging to Papine", and "Patent by Brayne Part of Mona" – the latter including a box marked "Mona". The Brayne referenced would be Major Richard Brayne who received extensive land grants in the area during the 1660s.

Comparison of the damaged 1804 map with a June 1831 map by James Dudley, Surveyor, seems to put the building still known as Mona Great House at the location of the earlier box marked Mona. Also relevant is a reference, in an early historical guide to the Mona campus,

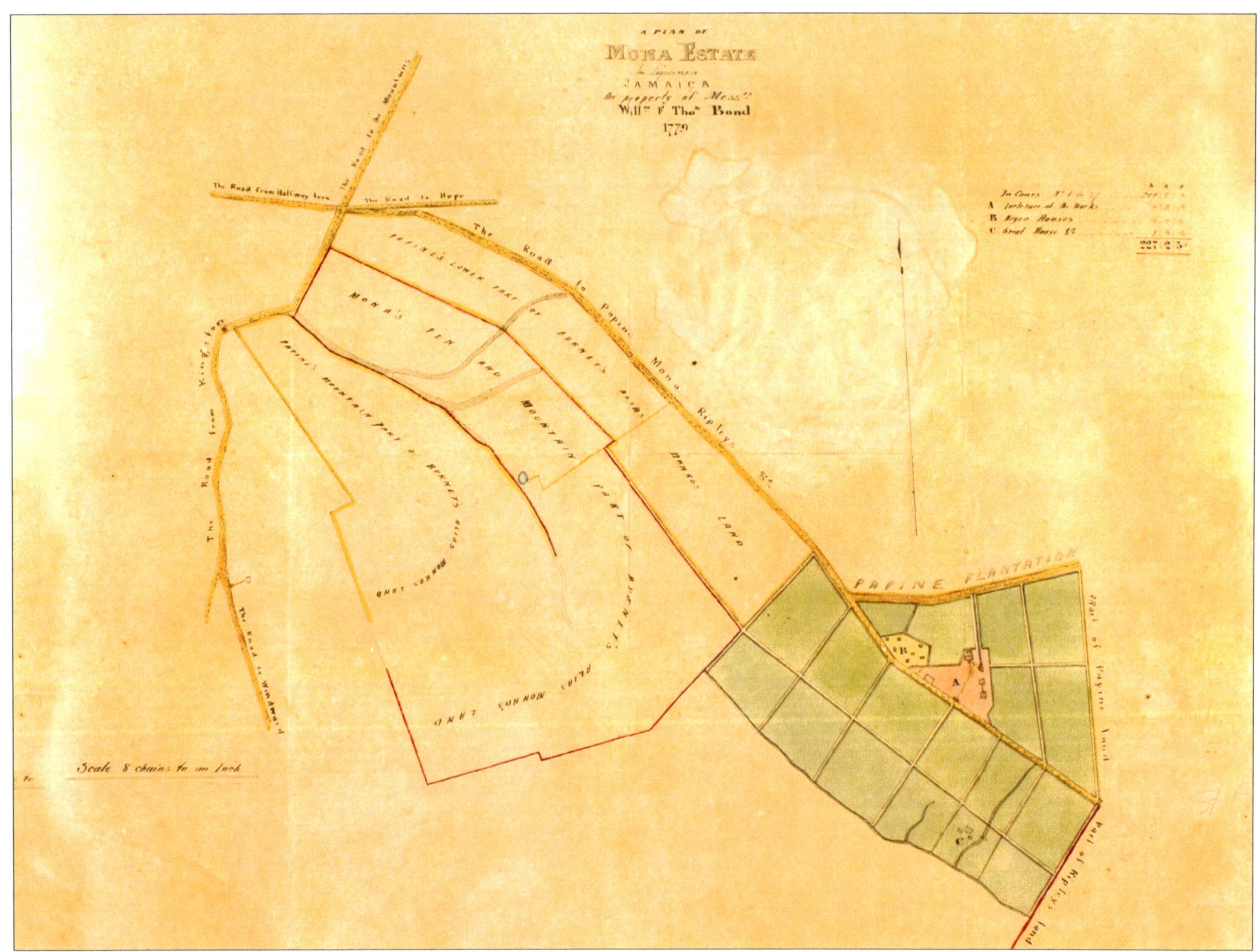

1779 survey map of Mona Estate

Mona Estate in 1797

A 1797 Chancery Court case lists the following Mona Estate buildings and furnishings:

. . . a Mansion House, Overseers House, a Kitchen and Iron Store, a new Boiling House laid with rangers and Molasses Cistern leaded and Acquaduct of fifty one Arches for carrying the water to the Wheel, a Mill House and liquor receiver leaded containing five hundred gallons, a Necessary House, a Compleat Mill House, a Copper containing about two hundred and fifty gallon. One Ditto one hundred and twenty – One Ditto sixty six – Ten Ditto one hundred and ten – One Ditto ninety – and one Ditto sixty – two Clarifiers containing three hundred and fifty Gallon each, a water receiver leaded containing three hundred Gallons and four Ceder coolers. A Curing House with Rangers and platt form, one Molasses cistern of one thousand two hundred gallons leaded, a Mill House, fourteen fermenting cisterns Eight Hundred gallons each, a Mixing Cistern of one thousand eight hundred Gallons and two Dunder Cisterns and Tank. A low wine still of seven hundred gallons with worm [?] to suit, a Rum Still of four hundred gallons with worm [?] to suit, a low wine Butt of five hundred gallons, two copper pumps and six rum and low wine Cans, a Rum Store, three Rum Butts of five hundred Gallons each with three brass cocks. Two crutched [?] trash houses, a Carpenters shop and shed for carriages, a Horse Stable and wash house under one Roof, Hot House containing a Hall and two rooms and Piazza and about one thousand and fifty acres of land in canes, pastures and otherwise and of one hundred and sixty five slaves thereon and a large and considerable number of Cattle and other live stock upon the said Plantation . . .

to a 1681 plan of Mona Estate comprising 40 acres, with a house at the present site, apparently belonging to a Benjamin Brayne. This map has not been located. The guide also mentions a 1684 Bochart and Knollis map of Jamaica, showing land granted to Benjamin Brayne. However, the link – if any – between Richard Brayne, one of the soldiers granted land in the area in the 1660s, and Benjamin Brayne in the 1680s is not clear.

The present Mona Great House lies to the west of the UWI, and while clearly not the original house, it sits on an older foundation. A 1990 Jamaica National Heritage Trust report notes that a complex of stone walls under the present floorboards reflects an earlier structure. Artefacts associated with the walls range in age from 1660 to 1800, including a pre-1750 Tippet pipe fragment. Brick foundations abutting on the stone walls are said to represent a later stage of building, probably in the period 1790 to 1830 – a period consistent with the 1831 map reference to the Mona Great House in its present location, at a time when the estate was owned by William and Thomas Bond and their heirs.

During the intervening period, references on maps in the National Library of Jamaica collection clearly indicate the Mona Estate great house in the area now called College Common, on the UWI property at the base of the Long Mountain. A 1779 plan of Mona Estate, already the property of Messrs William and Thomas Bond, shows a great house and outhouses on 8 acres of land. Its location is about 12 chains as the crow flies, south of the gate to the Mona Works, across the Hermitage Road in the College Common area. The location is north of the August Town Gully, which is a major feature of the landscape, close to another narrow gully which runs perpendicular to the larger channel. On the plan, a bridge appears to span the smaller gully, close to the house. A surviving substantial brick and cut-stone bridge which spans the August Town Gully next to the present Long Mountain Road on College Common, west of the marked house location, is not shown on the 1779 map. It has been pencilled on to a 1785 survey map of the estate, but by whom and at what point is not clear. Historian and cartographer David Buisseret, who taught at the UWI in the 1960s and 1970s and authored an early historical guide to the campus, suggests that heavy carts laden with bagasse (the trash from ground sugar cane) may have crossed the bridge on their way into the hills to dump their loads.

The site of this great house has not been ascertained, though Professor Buisseret recalls

Old stone and brick bridge over the August Town Gully, on Long Mountain Road

that he and UWI Professor Emeritus Edward Baugh had found broken pottery in a bank at Baugh's home on Long Mountain Close in College Common during the 1960s after heavy rains. There are old stone walls in the garden of the same house.

So the explanation of the disparity appears to be that there were three houses connected to the estate. The first, dating back into the late 1600s, was abandoned for whatever reason. A second was built at College Common, near to the sugar works, and certainly was in use in the last quarter of the eighteenth century. Then the estate owners, seemingly the Bonds, decided to relocate the estate house, and the present Mona Great House was built over the foundations of the seventeenth-century house. The present house has, of course, also seen many changes since the nineteenth century.

The entrance to the Mona Works yard was on the road leading from Kingston to Hermitage and Ripleys, the present August Town area and beyond. The Mona sugar mill was turned, after the mid-1700s, by a water-wheel fed by the aqueduct running across from the Papine Estate. The mill sent cane juice, in season, to a boiling and curing house, where it was gradually processed into muscovado sugar, and to the distillery, where it was made into rum and stored in a strongly built room to age until ready for sale. There were stables and livestock pens, and houses for the overseer and bookkeeper, and a village for the Negro slaves.

Many threads came together in creating the Mona Estate. There was the unclear Brayne connection, alluded to earlier. Part of the estate

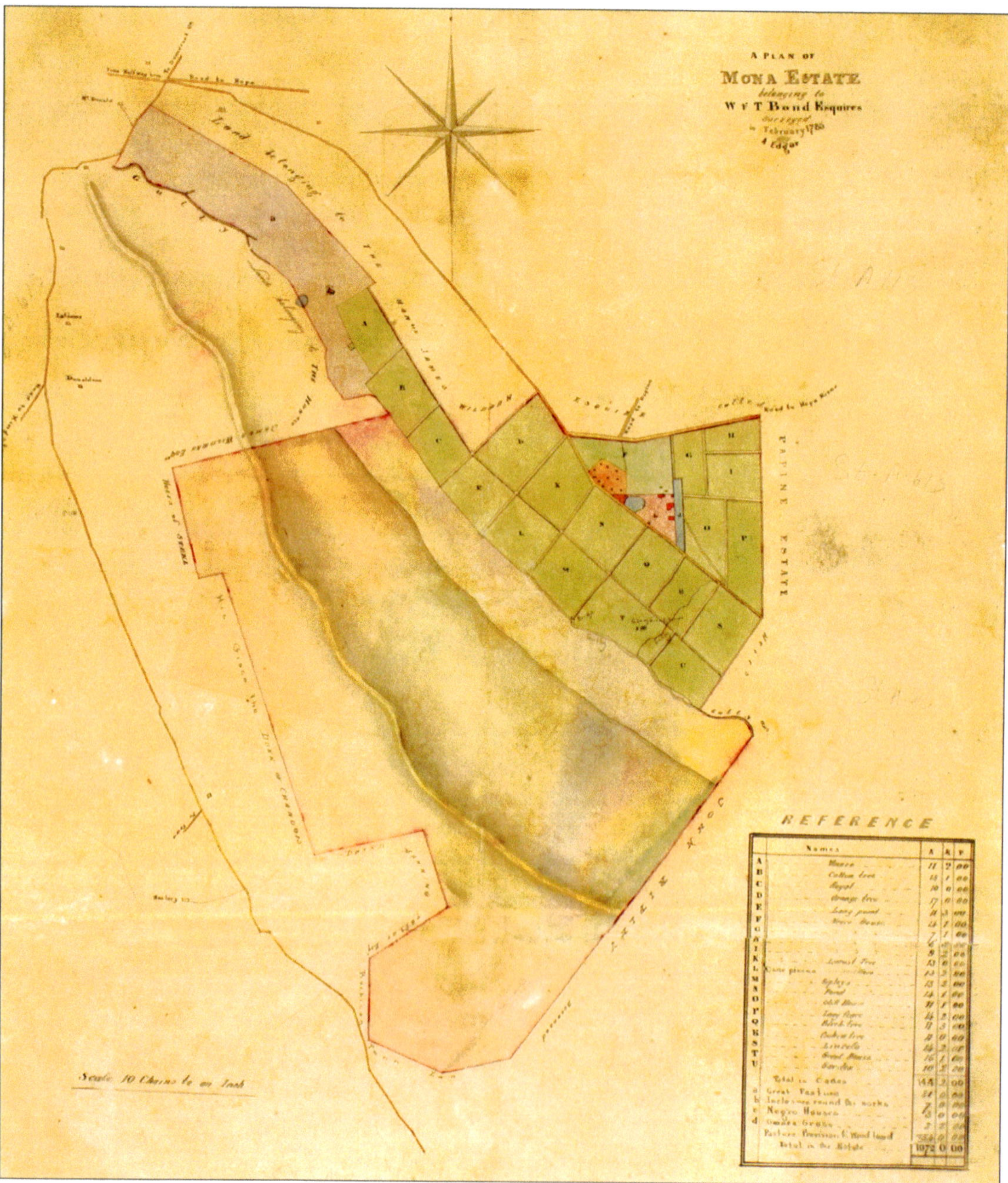

1785 plan of Mona Estate

Date on Mona still-house

Philip Pinnock, one of the owners of the Mona Estate

also once belonged to a property called Burnett's Penn, after George Burnett of Aberdeenshire, Scotland. By the early eighteenth century, the property was known as "Yeamans". Eleanor Angelina Yeamans inherited it in 1754 and sold it to Philip and Grace Pinnock. A 1845 document on the origin of the Hope water supply notes that around 1757, "Philip Pennock [*sic*] of St Andrew was seized of a plantation or sugar-work called Yeomans [*sic*] which is now called Mona Estate".

Pinnock, a planter and politician, who in 1754 owned nearly 4,000 acres in St Andrew, disputed with Thomas Hope Elletson – a descendant of Major Richard Hope and then owner of nearby Hope Estate – over rights to the water from the Hope River before they came to an agreement on the aqueduct scheme. He would later have a public falling-out with Thomas's brother, Lieutenant Governor Roger Hope Elletson, over a money bill in the House of Assembly. Pinnock owned Mona when the estate's still-house was erected in 1759. The capstone on one of the remaining arches of the building carries the date incised in the rock.

Around 1767, the plantation was sold with slaves and stock to John Kennion. In short order, Kennion had mortgaged the estate to William and Thomas Bond – the first, a prominent merchant, his brother a magistrate. The 1779 estate plan refers to the Bonds as the proprietors of the estate, and they or their heirs appear to have remained in charge well into the nineteenth century.

Never one of the great sugar-producing properties, Mona Estate would nonetheless have been seriously affected by the ending of the slave trade in 1807, the end of slavery in 1838, the gradual ending of protected status in the British market by 1854, and increasing competition from European beet-sugar during the last quarter of the century.

Sales of sugar and rum were supplemented by sales of livestock – including cattle and sheep – and rental of land to labourers after 1838. Estate accounts for 1835, submitted by estate attorney Charles Anderson and overseer John Copland, note 78 hogsheads of sugar and 34 puncheons of rum shipped to England, four head of cattle sold locally, and rents from land. Livestock was still important on any estate – cattle to draw wagons, carts and ploughs, and mules and horses for riding.

By the 1860s, the estate had been taken over by Lewis Verley, who clearly set out to make a go of it, despite the drawbacks. In 1864, the Mirrlees and Watson foundry in Scotland drew a plan of a new overshot water-wheel ordered by Verley of Mona Estate. (The plan and the water-wheel are illustrated overleaf.)

During the late 1800s, when sugar prices were low, the estate appears to have balanced its sugar and rum production to best effect. Estate accounts for 1879 to 1881, quoted by C.B. Lewis in "Some Notes on the Mona Estate", show an average annual production of 67 hogsheads of sugar and 200 puncheons of rum, with some 101 free "coolies" employed monthly during the period. The estate's distillery or still-house, with its attached rum store, would have been well used. An 1884 *Return of Sugar Estates and Other Properties in Jamaica* notes how the estate, then 1,072 acres, was used: 195

1864 Mirrlees & Watson plan of a water-wheel for Mona Estate

The overshot wheel furnishing power for grinding

Some Representative Data for Mona Estate (Compiled from Returns of Slaves, Accounts Produce, Maps, Almanack, *Handbook of Jamaica* etc.)

	Acreage (hogshead)	Sugar Prod. (puncheon)	Rum Production	Livestock Sold	Stock	Rents	Workforce	Owner
1754								Eleanor Yeamans
1757								Philip Pinnock
1767								John Kennion
1775		182	54					Wm. & Thos. Bond
1785	1,072 (144 cane; 827 grass, woodland etc)						approx. 172 slaves	
1817		106	37	16 cattle – £207	118		187 slaves	Heirs to Wm. Bond
1826		120	63	9 cattle – £113			177 slaves (77 m.; 100 f.)	"
1832		112	50	8 cattle – £128	75		165 slaves (69 m.; 96 f.)	"
1844	1,372	26	13	9 old cattle – £42.15		£107.0.3		
1880	1,072	135	109				approx. 101 E. Indians	Louis Verley (1858)
1908[a]	953 (30 cane)	25	20					Eliza Verley
1914[b]	1,068				200			Kingston General Commissioners

[a]The 1910 *Handbook of Jamaica* lists Mona under sugar estates with 953 acres, and under grazing pens with 1,848 acres – both for 1908–9.

[b]The Kingston General Commissioners bought 2,664 acres, 24 perches – one property comprising Mona, Papine, Hermitage. The 1919 *Handbook of Jamaica* provides the Mona information listed here.

The Mona sugar plantation

in cane, 10 in guinea grass, 65 in common pasture, 802 in wood and ruinate. Verley extended his property to include nearby Latimer Pen, purchased in 1870, Papine, purchased in 1871, and Hermitage Pen, which he bought in portions, between 1885 and 1891 – eventually taking his holdings in the area to 2,664 acres.

Verley's widow Eliza was the last private owner of the estate, and the 1910 *Handbook of Jamaica* gives the last record of sugar production at Mona, for the year 1908: 35 hogsheads of sugar and 30 puncheons of rum from 30 acres of cane. Mona was the last sugar estate operating in the parish of St Andrew.

Papine Estate

On Papine Estate, by contrast, sugar production had ended from 1880. Records relating to the estate have been traced back to 1756 by Geoffrey Yates, in an article for the Jamaica Historical Society. He notes that Colonel Alexander Grant, originally of Achoyname and Arndilly in Scotland, bought half of a property called Burnett's Pen for £2,000. This land, north of Hope Common, became the nucleus of Papine Plantation. A later document in relation to the 1757 development of the Hope water supply, notes that "Alexander Grant and Walter Grant were seized of Papine Plantation".

Another Grant, Nathaniel, a churchwarden, is mentioned in relation to a 1767 agreement between Roger Hope Elletson and the owners of Mona and Papine, aimed at allowing inhabitants of Kingston to benefit from spare water from the Hope River.

Grant clearly added to his property over the years. A 1774 survey of "Alexander Lindo's mountain situate at Hope River" by P.M. Smellie carries the following notation along a boundary line: "Boundary to Mr Lindo and Papin [*sic*]. Gerand Snow to Alexander Grant 90 acres by deed dated 19th of May 1766, now belonging to Papin Estate."

Alexander Grant died in Jamaica in 1779. Before that, in 1774, the transfer of Papine Estate from Grant to William Jackson is noted on a survey map in the National Library of Jamaica collection: "Alexander Grant to William Jackson, 944 acres, 2 roods, 34 perches in the parish of St Andrew, surveyed 2 November 1774 by John Henderson, Surveyor." The same map notes that the adjoining Mona Estate belongs to John Kennion Esquire, and formerly Philip Pinnock Esquire.

The 1774 plan indicates the location of "The Gutter" – the old name for the aqueduct which brought water across the Hope, Papine and Mona estates to run their sugar mills. It also shows the Papine Works and house as well as the Mona Works, located along an estate road which diverged north from the road dividing the Papine and Mona estates, then ran to the east. The works, of which only the wheel-house remains relatively intact, appears to have comprised three buildings: the wheel-house into which the aqueduct ran, turning the wheel and thereby the mill rollers and crushing cane brought into the adjoining mill-house; the boiling and curing house just south; and the L-shaped distillery fronting on the estate road which ran to the great house.

A subsequent survey by Robert Baugh Junior, drawn in 1834, four years before slaves were emancipated, shows the works in a compound more than eight acres in extent, and the Great House and Garden on more than 10 acres. The overseer's house, and old and new Negro houses, are also identified. The scale on this plan would place the great house some 22 chains due east-north-east of the Papine Works.

The location of the great house has not been confirmed though Thera Edwards, in a floral history of the campus, estimates that "the area extending from the east side of Irvine [Hall] to the UTCWI [United Theological College of the West Indies] was occupied by the Papine great house and its gardens".

A graphic description of the great house, in its day, may be found in Lady Maria Nugent's 1801–5 diary of her sojourn in Jamaica when her husband, General George Nugent, was Lieutenant Governor:

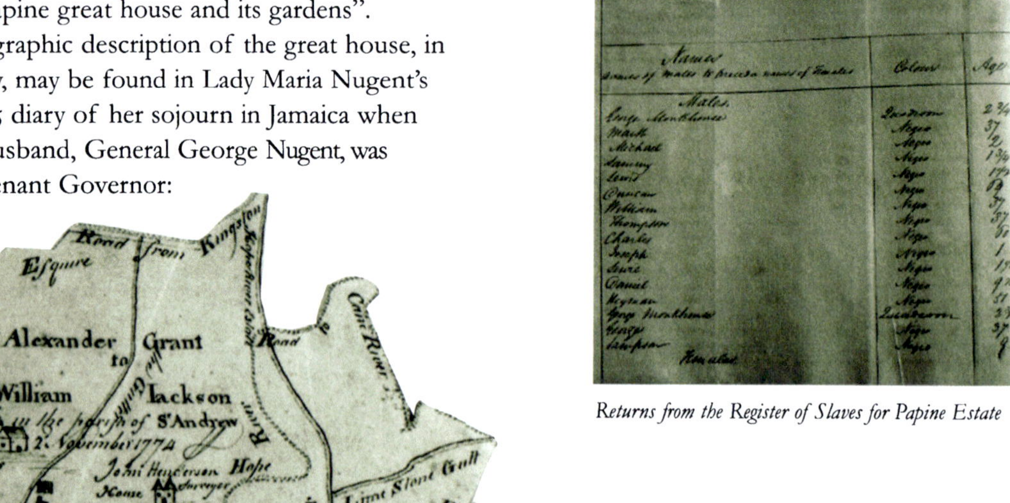

Returns from the Register of Slaves for Papine Estate

1774 survey map of Papine Estate, by John Henderson

> Drove to Mr Hutchinson's place, called the Papine estate. A large party of gentlemen, and a grand cavalcade of all descriptions. All sorts of meats and fruits at breakfast. See a fine bamboo walk afterwards, reaching from one end of the garden to the other. Every ten or twelve feet there is a cocoa-nut tree, as a pillar to support the feathering bamboo. Nothing could well be more beautiful. The bread-fruit

Sugar and rum en route, pictured on an early postcard

Papine wheel-house ruin

tree is here in great perfection. The jackfruit tree is like an enormous pumpkin, growing on the trunk, as it is too heavy for the boughs. There is also an infinite variety of beautiful flowers; in short, the garden is the best and most curious I have yet seen. – The situation of the house is bad; it lies low, and it is shut out from the sea breeze, by what is called the Long Mountain, and from the land breeze, by a range of mountains, under which the house is placed. Mr Hutchinson is a quiet, awkward Scotchman, and so overcome by the honour we have done him, that it is quite distressing to see the poor man.

About 10 we drove to the Hope Estate. We took a cross road, through a sugar plantation, or rather a cane-piece, as it is called; a negro man running before the carriage, to open the gates . . .

Mr Hutchinson's name notwithstanding, it appears that Papine was already owned by James Beckford Wildman. Certainly this is indicated on a plan of neighbouring Mona Estate done in February 1785, when William and Thomas Bond were in control there. Subsequent survey diagrams – of Hope Estate, done by E. McGeachy in 1826 and of Papine Estate itself in 1834 by Robert Baugh, Junior – also note Wildman's ownership of Papine.

By 1843, with slavery abolished, Mr Wildman was gaining some additional income by selling a part-share of the water running through the aqueduct which bisected his property and fed his sugar mill, to the military establishment at Up Park Camp. A long and detailed letter from W. Barron to the Duke of Buckingham and Chandos regarding the state of his properties in Jamaica, chiefly Hope Estate, notes: "The military post at Up Park Camp near Kingston is supplied with water from the division of the River belonging to Papine Estate, for which that property receives £400 a year." Mr Wildman appears to have also sold water to the Anglican bishop.

A subsequent letter regarding the Hope Estate, in 1867, also mentions the sale of water:

> It is true that Mr Wildman, the owner of Papine Estate gets £500 a year from Government for the use of the surplus of his share of this very water, and that therefore a like sum might be reasonably expected for that of Hope, but times have much altered since that bargain was made, and I have it from good authority that Mr Wildman is willing to supply the water required at even a less rate than £300 . . .

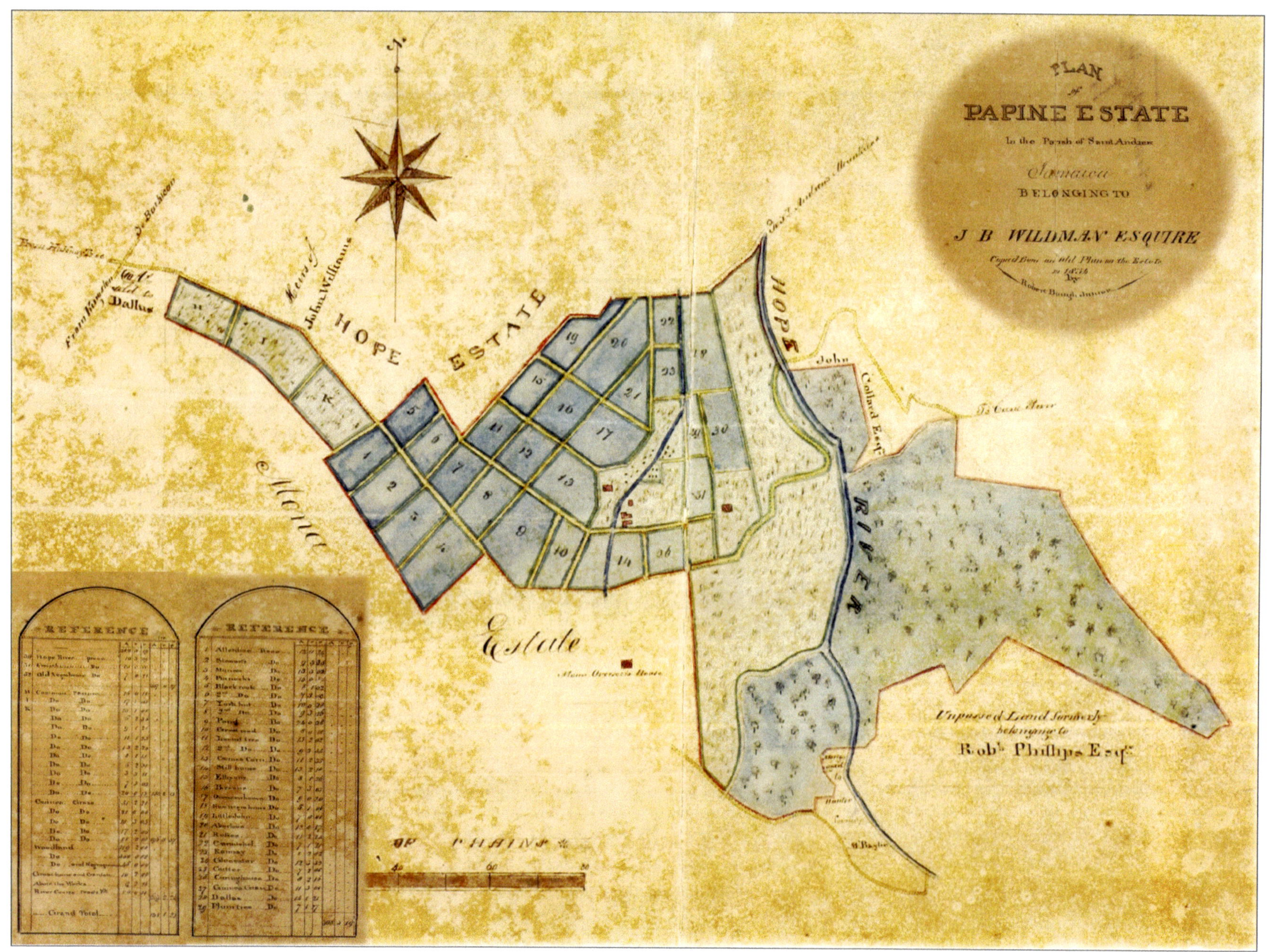

1834 survey of Papine Estate

Carting logwood – an early postcard

In May 1871, James Lushington Wildman, the English based grandson of the first J.B. Wildman, sold Papine to Louis Verley who was already owner of the neighbouring Mona Estate. By 1880, Papine was no longer listed as one of St Andrew's sugar estates.

African Ancestors

Africans were first brought to Jamaica as slaves by the Spanish, in small numbers and apparently as body servants. Many of them were freed and formed the nucleus of the Maroon community when the Spanish came under English attack in 1655. Subsequently, the English imported tens of thousands of West African slaves, across the Middle Passage, to work on their plantations. The early Africans on the site would most likely have been servants to some of the early settlers, and slaves working on the Papine and Mona estates.

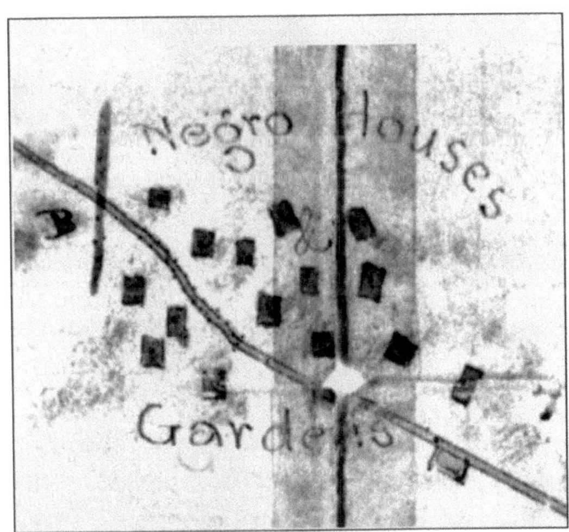

Detail from survey drawing, "Division of Water Above Hope Works"

In their heyday, both estates exceeded 1,000 acres, though only a fraction of that would have been in cane; the balance was used for livestock, pasture, woodland, housing and provision grounds for the slaves. An unpublished manuscript written in the 1920s by Winifred Cousins notes: "Every sugar estate was also a cattle-ranch, the livestock being as a rule about two-thirds as many as the slaves."

The numbers of enslaved persons on each estate would have varied with time, but seems to have remained under 200. A "List of Negroes on St Andrew Estates, 1783" includes 172 at Mona and 187 at Papine.

Slave returns tell us the names of many of these individuals and we have some sense of where and how they lived. Estate maps indicate the position of the Papine and Mona slave villages. A February 1779 plan of Mona Estate shows 200 acres in cane, and identifies the works enclosure, the great house and its environs, and the Negro houses. A subsequent 1831 survey map, based on a 1785 plan, shows approximately 28 dots in the area identified as the Mona slave village, though it is difficult to know whether the surveyor intended the number to be taken as an accurate representation or

Ackee groves are a major botanical marker for slave villages

simply as an indication that there were several huts in the area.

The Papine slave village is identified on the 1834 plan of the Papine Estate. An undated, but probably late-eighteenth-century plan, detailing the division of water taken from the Hope River and used to turn the mills on the Hope, Mona and Papine estates, also shows Negro houses and gardens on the Papine Estate. Some 15 small squares are inked in around the aqueduct, north-west of the Papine Works. And a 1915 survey map of Kingston identifies an area west of the Papine Works as "Nigger House Corner".

The information from the maps and plans is supported by botanical markers – the ackee groves near West Road, on the former Papine Estate; and in and around the Chemistry parking lot, site of the old Mona village. The fairly young trees are presumably descendants of early ackee trees, whose fruit would have gone into the cooking pots of slaves living in their shadow. There are also quite a number of mango trees in these areas – mango being another of the fruit trees cultivated in groves near to slave villages. Others included coconut, citrus, starapple, gourd, breadfruit and banana, according to a listing in Thera Edwards' "Floral History of the Mona Campus". She notes that gardens would also have been planted with such fruit, vegetables and ground provisions as pineapple, melon, peas, passionfruit, castor bean, cassava, okra, yam and chocho.

These would have been supplemented with the produce of provision grounds allocated on marginal estate lands. This produce, including coco, arrowroot, pumpkin, sweet potato, melon, plantain and banana, ginger, corn, sugar cane, and even cotton, also provided a cash income when sold at Sunday market. James Hakewill, in an introduction to his 1825 *Picturesque Tour of the Island of Jamaica*, commented in grander terms: "[N]early the whole of the markets of Jamaica are supplied with every species of vegetables and fruit by the overplus of the negro's produce, by which traffic they acquire considerable riches." Hakewill, who spent two years visiting planters and painting his picturesque views on major estates around the island, argued that this and other concessions made the lot of local slaves, in general, equal or superior to that of the working classes in western Europe.

"A New and General Plan of the Hope Estate in the Parishes of Kingston and St Andrew", drawn in 1826 by Edward McGeachy, places the Papine Estate "Negroe Grounds" along the line of the aqueduct, below the Papine reservoir which lay close to "Hope Lane" and which is now under the University Hospital.

And it is generally conceded that slaves on the Mona Estate would have had their provision grounds on the higher slopes of the Long Mountain.

Food aside, the lifestyles of the slaves would have depended significantly on the season of the year, with its attendant duties in the cane fields and at the mill; on the level of latitude allowed by the estate owner, his overseers and other hirelings; and on the type of work allocated, whether in the house, the field or at a skilled occupation such as cooperage, carpentry or blacksmithing. Slaves who were expert in

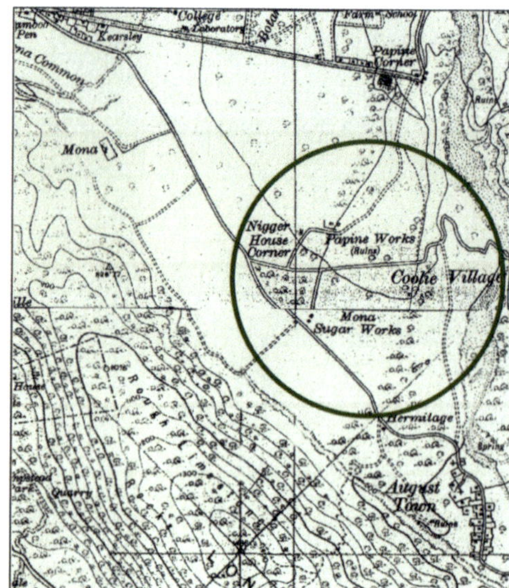

Detail from 1915 survey map of the Kingston area

Women carrying provisions, in an early postcard

Drawing of slaves cutting cane on a sugar estate

Artefacts found during a 1989 archaeological dig

some area of value to the estate might gain improved working conditions and earning opportunities.

Special tasks, such as the building of the aqueduct, would have brought additional back-breaking work. Slaves on the estates would have had to bring rocks, gravel and sand from the river as well as labour over the construction, breaking and smoothing the stones, and binding the stone and imported red brick with powdered limestone.

In 1989, the Papine slave village site was the subject of an excavation exercise, during which UWI History students dug test pits at randomly selected sites in the old "Negro Yard" as identified on the 1834 plan of Papine Estate.

Three foundations were exposed and a variety of fragments were collected. Participants theorized that a variation in the number of artefacts found, from pit to pit, might indicate some ranking among the slaves. Items found included:

Pit 2: Tapestry needle; chalk piece (white stone); canine tooth and tooth fragments; shards of glazed stoneware; shards of patterned redware; fragments of drinking goblets; clay pipe shards; red brick used in foundation; nails.

Pit 3: Bone fragments; mortar for constructing houses; reconstructed mocha bowl; bits of blue transfer print plate; bits of shell-edged plates (both blue and green); metal bolt; eighteenth-century lock; metal barrel bands; metal fragments.

Pit 4: Piece of a wooden whistle; neck and base of wine bottle dated around 1807 by its shape; metal hooks; green glass bottle fragments; clay pipe shards (used throughout the slavery period); old iron key.

Charcoal remnants were found in all the pits, but most in Pit 2 where a circular hole, found eight inches below the surface, had been dug for cooking, indicating an inside fire. Slaves often cooked outside in the open or in sheds attached to their houses.

Quantities of wattle and daub were also excavated, indicating that the sides of the houses were made using it. A card from a library exhibition on the excavation notes: "The flooring would seem to have been made of compacted stone, finished with a type of lime wash. No roofing materials were found, indicating that roofs were constructed of perishable materials – most likely thatch or trash."

After the abolition of slavery, many former slaves appear to have remained on the estates, at least initially – tenure in their homes guaranteed by labour on the estate and by payment of rent. In a dispatch on "The Labouring Population in the West Indies", dated in the late 1830s, Stephen Bourne reports to G.H. Darling his understanding that on the Mona and Papine estates, "the people are doing very well, and that the price of labour is by no means extravagant". Another dispatch to the Colonial Office, dated May 11, 1839, notes disputes occurring between plantation managers and Negroes in St Andrew:

> I can see no general indisposition on the part of the negroes to labour, and the right of the landlord to rent is undisputed; but notwithstanding this, it is my painful duty to state, that much dissatisfaction exists in the minds of the negroes, and that they are far from being reconciled to this present lot, the causes of which are, the frequent rooting up of their provisions under very slight pretences; the very capricious tenure allowed them of houses and grounds, and the exceedingly repulsive manner in which it is attempted to charge them with rent; for instance, a man paying at a rate of 3s.4d. weekly, for house and ground, is also charged an additional sum for his wife's use of the ground, generally 1s.8d. weekly, and a further charge is made against every member of the family who is able to work, of from 1s.8d. to 10d. weekly.

Early postcard shows "Coolie Residence"

Asian Indentureship

Following the abolition of slavery, many West Indian governments sought to mitigate labour shortages by immigration and indentureship schemes. In the end, the largest numbers came from Asia, especially from India. Starting in the 1840s, and continuing until the early 1900s, over 400,000 East Indian immigrants entered the British West Indies, some 33,000 of them coming to Jamaica. A 1992 "Report on the Preservation and Development of the Historic Features of the Mona Campus" notes that Jaghi the Indian, whose tomb lies close to Taylor Hall, grew rice near the Mona–Papine boundary, and makes reference to a "Coolie village" (*circa* 1900), mostly under Irvine Hall.

"Coolie Girls" in an early postcard

Tombstone west of Taylor Hall

Shed Lane – once a semi-public road dividing the Papine and Mona estates and leading past Hope River to "Hall's Delight"

Map detail showing Road to Hall's Delight

Mr Allan Rae, whose father was Manager and, later, Commandant of Gibraltar Camp (located on a section of the present UWI campus during World War II) noted many East Indians living in the Papine area when he lived at Gibraltar Camp. In an interview during 2001, he said that his sister had once seen an Indian man pinned to the ground between the long horns of a bull, near to the present University Hospital gate. Certainly livestock and small crop farming took place on sections of the old Papine and Mona estates after they went out of business as sugar plantations and were sold to the Kingston water authorities.

And sugar estate returns from the early 1880s note that the Verleys, the last private individuals owning the Mona property, employed an average of 101 free "coolies" monthly. A 1915 survey map of Kingston shows an area called "Coolie Village" in what would have been the north-eastern portion of the Mona Estate, close to the road to Hall's Delight; and there are references to a "Coolie village" on the site of the present Irvine Hall.

There is also reference, in an earlier historical guide to the UWI Mona campus, to fields where Jeng Jeng grew tobacco. Reverend Easton Lee, who has researched the Jamaican Chinese experience, recalls Chinese living in the Papine area early in the twentieth century.

Some 5,000 Chinese came to Jamaica as indentured labourers during the second half of the nineteenth century, again as part of the effort to find additional labour. Many of them were apparently Hakka people from South China.

Shed Lane

Survey drawings going back to 1779, and perhaps before, show a road from Half Way Tree running to the Hope Estate, with an offshoot running between Papine and Mona and, eventually, on to Hope River, Hall's Delight, Dallas Castle and Cane River. This section of road that divided the main body of the Papine and Mona estates would at some point become known as Shed Lane – possibly a derivation of Shade Lane. Up to 1950, Shed Lane ran diagonally across the then University College of the West Indies (UCWI) site from Mona Road, opposite the Mona Reservoir, to what is now the Irvine Hall gate. Columns on either side of the gate may hark back to the road's early days. Shed Lane was cut short during the first phase of building of the UCWI, later the UWI, campus.

Near the Mona Reservoir, another offshoot of the public road took a more south-easterly course towards Hermitage and Ripleys – what is now the August Town area. This road, which ran in front of the Mona Works, is now known as Hermitage Road and is the main approach to the Mona campus of the UWI.

The Aqueduct

The brick and cut-stone aqueduct, which bisects the landscape across large parts of the UWI Mona campus, carried water drawn from the Hope River and then divided to feed the sugar works of several estates.

An undated diagram in the National Library of Jamaica details the division of water drawn from the river into a 5-foot gutter, which was then divided above the Hope Works. A section – originally a wooden gutter – fed the works and another carried water for the Papine, Mona and Ripley estates. Just below Hope Lane, now Hope Road, the water was again divided, with a portion going to Ripleys, a second portion directly to the Papine and then the Mona Works, and a third portion feeding a Papine reservoir, now buried under the University Hospital of the West Indies complex.

According to the diagram, the aqueduct covered a total distance of 4,550 feet from the point where it crossed Hope Lane onto the old Papine estate, to the Mona Works. The flow of water into and out of the aqueduct was controlled by run-offs and sluice gates, as well as by valves. Historian Dr Sultana Afroz, writing on Mona campus features, notes: "To control the volume of water in the gutter and the dam, especially in times of flooding, a number of valves were placed at different points. The valves were operated by turning the wheel left or right to increase or decrease the flow of water."

The diagram charts the course of the aqueduct through the Papine and Mona estates, noting the relative position of the sugar works, the slave/worker villages, and the Papine "Negroe Grounds". The 1774 survey of the Papine Estate, at the time when the property was sold by Alexander Grant to William Jackson, refers to the aqueduct as "The Gutter".

Development of the aqueduct system is generally credited to Roger Hope Elletson, a descendant of Major Richard Hope who was granted the Hope Estate in the 1660s. However, the idea of using the water to turn the estate mill seems to have originated with his brother Thomas.

The history is recorded in an 1845 Colonial Office report, which notes the 1752 passage of "An act to enable Thomas Hope Elletson, esquire, to take up a sufficient quantity of water for turning mills for grinding of sugar-canes out of Hope River, in the parish of St Andrew, and to convey the same through lands of divers persons to the said plantation of the said Thomas Hope Elletson, called Hope Plantation, in the said parish". However, disputes between Hope Elletson and persons holding lands below Hope, especially the proprietors of Papine and Mona, caused the passage, in 1757, of another act, to make the first act "more effectual". The intention was to clarify the rights of all the interested parties to the water conveyed in the aqueduct. The result was to confirm, to Hope Elletson, his heirs and assigns, one-third of the stream of water conveyed from the river by the aqueduct; another third to the owners of Papine and Mona estates, in equal shares; and the balance to the lands between the river and the Hope Estate. The aqueduct system in the present Hope Gardens is dated 1758, the

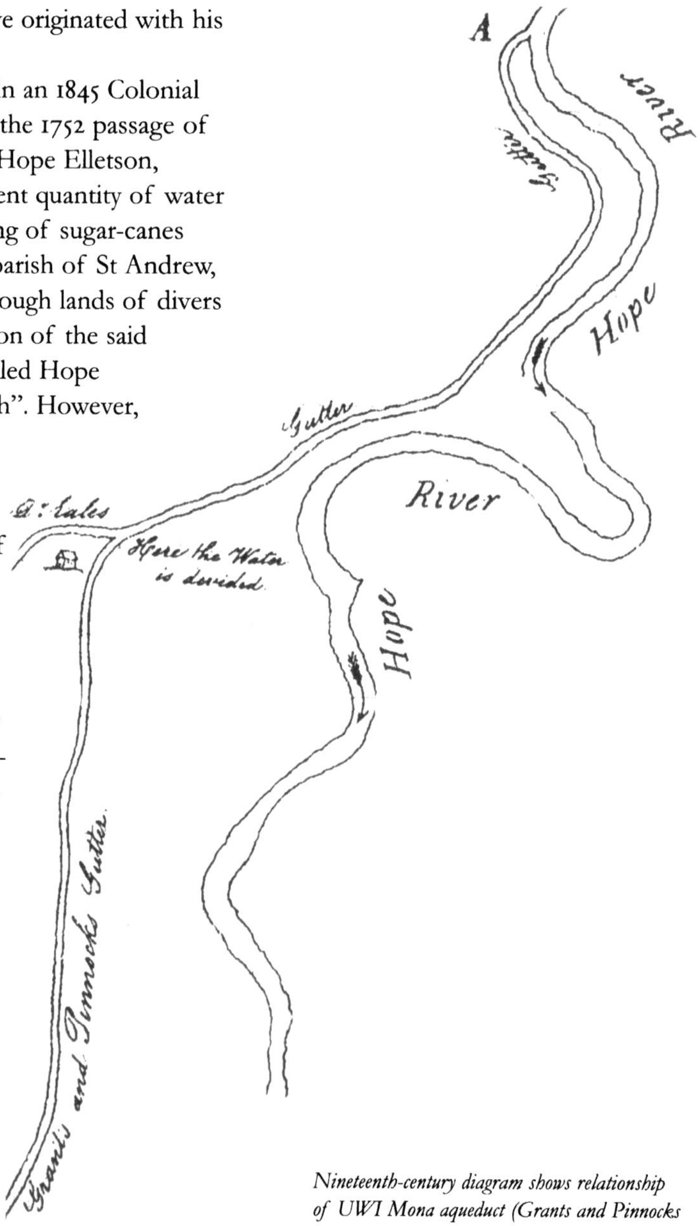

Nineteenth-century diagram shows relationship of UWI Mona aqueduct (Grants and Pinnocks Gutter) to the Hope Estate aqueduct and the point where the water was drawn from the Hope River (Colonial Office report, 1845)

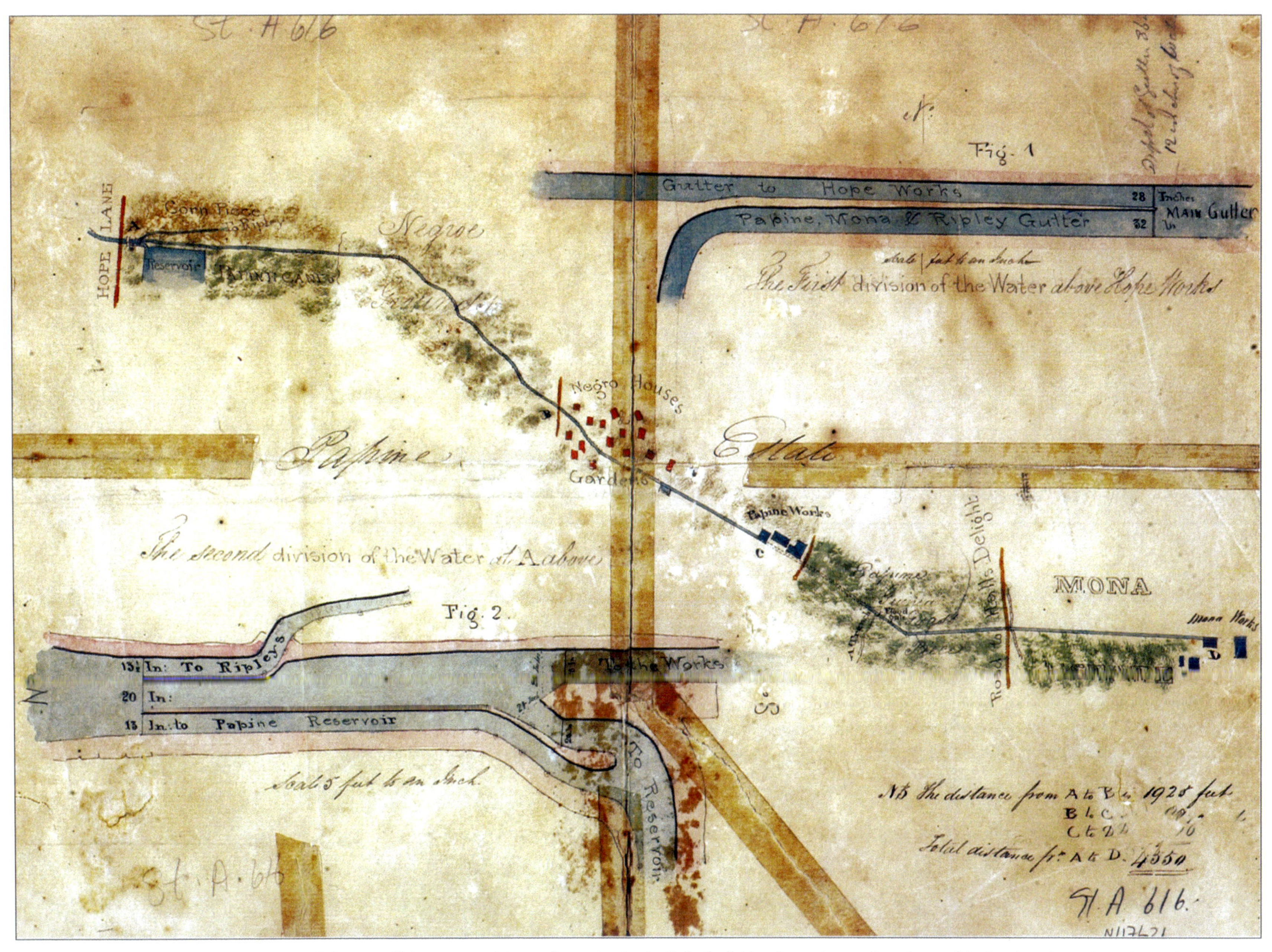

This undated survey drawing describes the length of the Papine and Mona portion of the aqueduct; engineering details for the division of water between the various participating plantations, prior to the stretch shown, are at top right (Division above Hope Works, following intake from the Hope River) and bottom left (Second Division)

following year. By 1767, based on a number of deeds between the parties, the right to four-ninths of the stream vested in the owners of Hope Estate, three-ninths in the owners of Papine and two-ninths in the owner of Mona.

Thomas Hope Elletson died around this time and his younger brother Roger, Lieutenant Governor and Commander-in-Chief of the island, agreed with Peter Farnell, Custos of Kingston, and John Collard and Nathaniel Grant, churchwardens, on July 10, 1767,

> to give and grant to the inhabitants of Kingston all the benefit and advantage of the said stream of water so conveyed by means of the said aqueduct to the said Hope Plantation, and for that purpose to permit and suffer such persons as should be appointed, on behalf of the town of Kingston, provided that nothing was done to undermine the rights of Elletson, Grant and Pinnock, their heirs or assigns, from enjoying their streams of water as before.

According to a historical account put out by the National Water Commission, in 1766 Elletson gave Kingston the surplus water from his property and constructed an open conduit into the town at his own expense. The water ran along Elletson Road to branches at Duke, King and Orange Streets. However the concession was cancelled after Elletson's death through the intervention of his attorneys, his widow and her new husband, the Duke of Chandos. Later, after their only child married the Duke of Buckingham, the estate would become the property of the Duke of Buckingham and Chandos. Elletson Flats and Chandos Place in Papine are two of the places in the area where these names are perpetuated.

The name of Hope lives on in Hope Road and the Hope Botanical Gardens. Mona gave its name to Mona Heights, and Papine to the village of the same name.

The 1961 history of the public water supply notes of Hope Elletson's aqueduct: "Completed in 1758, a portion of it, virtually untouched by time, still carries the branch supply from the Mona conduit to the Hope Filters . . ." The Papine and Mona sections have now been out of use for many decades.

The aqueduct runs from near the present-day hospital boundary, across the lawn adjoining Aqueduct Road, past an old tank, into the Papine wheel-house. The UWI's Ring Road development undoubtedly destroyed some ruins of the Papine Works.

After turning the Papine wheel, the aqueduct went underground into a cistern, reappearing many yards further on, inside of what is now the Ring Road. The National Library of Jamaica diagram on page 21 shows it reappearing, as a solid structure, about half-way between the Papine Works and Shed Lane, close to a trench, where a flood gate allowed water to reach the Papine Guinea Grass Piece. However the reality on the ground is that the aqueduct reappears east of the Assembly Hall just south of Shed Lane. From there, it runs straight to the overshot wheel of the Mona wheel-house, south-east of the University Chapel. Mona Works ruins are visible in the vicinity of the Senior Common Room and in the Oriental Garden. From there, the remaining water was led away south to a large pond. A brick sluice controlled the flow of water, which was used for nearby pasture and animals.

The aqueduct, made of cut-stone and brick

WINNING WATER RIGHTS

The takeover of the Hope, Papine and Mona estate lands by the water authorities began in the mid-1800s, at a time when slavery had been abolished in Jamaica, sugar was no longer king and many sugar estates were struggling.

Letters in the Stowe collection of papers related to the Hope Estate refer to extended negotiations between the owner of the estate, the Duke of Buckingham and Chandos, and the Kingston and Liguanea Waterworks Company, which had been incorporated in 1842.

A letter dated August 17, 1848, from the directors of the company, notes that two persons were in England negotiating to purchase the estate for the company. A history of the Water Commission, written in 1961 by W. Kirkpatrick, notes that the agreement was reached "to lease, pending purchase, part of his estate and rights to 4/9ths of the river flow". Survey map notations in 1849 record the conveyance of 634 acres of the Hope Estate by the Marquis of Chandos and Francis Richard, to the company. And the Marquis of Chandos, Buckingham's son, visited Jamaica in 1850 to conclude the deal whereby the company acquired 634 acres of land with buildings, conduits and works and the rights, for £6,215.

Water, for years available to residents of Kingston only through handcart sales, since the cancellation of the Elletson concession in the 1770s, now ran into Kingston at North Street, through a gutter. In 1871, shortly before the seat of government was finally shifted from Spanish Town to Kingston, the government bought out the Kingston and Liguanea Waterworks Company and vested control in a government board, the Kingston and Liguanea Water Works Commissioners.

The 1883 *Handbook of Jamaica* notes that Kingston and Liguanea were supplied with water from a four-ninths share of the flow of the Hope River which, in the driest season, was equal to about 5 cubic feet per second. The remaining five-ninths belonged to the owner of the Mona Estate – then Louis Verley who bought Mona in 1858, Papine in 1871 (having leased it since 1862) as well as nearby Hermitage and Latimers Pen.

In 1897, Law 24 created the Kingston General Commissioners to take over the water works as well as the Kingston Improvement Commission which had been established seven years earlier to set up a water borne sewerage system and pave city streets. In April 1914, an agreement with the trustees of Verley's widow, Eliza, conveyed to the Kingston General Commissioners and the Colonial Secretary of Jamaica, "all those estates, pens, pieces or parcels of land now forming one property known respectively as the Mona Estate (including the 'Mona Great House') the Papine Estate (including 'Papine Mountains') the 'Hermitage' and 'Latimer Pen' and all lands adjacent thereto respectively containing in the aggregate by survey 2,664 acres and 24 perches". With the land went the old sugar works and crucially, water rights to the remaining five-ninths of the flow of the Hope River; all at a price of £20,000.

Control of the water would come under the purview of the Kingston and St Andrew Corporation (1923) and the Water and Sewerage Board (1933) before the Water Commission was established by Law 34 of 1936. Though most projects ground to a halt during World War II, the Water Commission continued to undertake small supply projects for naval and military internment camps, "especially through a 10-inch main from the Hope Works to the large camp established on the Commission's property at Mona for the housing of the civilian population of Gibraltar who were evacuated to Jamaica when the situation in the Mediterranean appeared critical".

The Commission would continue to hold title to the land for the Government of Jamaica, even as the property was allocated for diverse uses.

Metal tank installed to supply Gibraltar Camp residents

An early drawing of the Hope River (Whisperings of the Caribbean, *1925*)

SAFE HAVEN DURING WORLD WAR II

Gibraltar Camp

When World War II got underway in 1939, the estates had been out of large-scale cultivation for some time, though there were people from the area living, grazing livestock and growing small crops on them. A part of the Mona Estate was leased to Mr Herman Taylor. In 1940, orders from England led to the identification of this estate as the site of an evacuation camp for first 4,000 and then 7,000 to 9,000 persons from the war-threatened British territories of Gibraltar and Malta. Mona, 7 miles by road from Kingston, was chosen because it had available space. It was also close to the services essential for establishing and maintaining a small township, which had to be constructed in the least possible time. And it had the advantage of being a government property in the name of the Colonial Secretary of Jamaica, under the immediate control of the Water Commission. Arrangements were concluded with the lessee, and people living on the site were apparently relocated to August Town.

A Public Works Department (PWD) interim report on work carried out on the camp from July 25, 1940 to January 31, 1941 reflects the urgency attached to the request for its establishment. For speed, a simple barracks design was chosen. Site survey and planning was completed in two days, and work began on clearing the site, constructing roads, erecting construction offices and stores, putting in water and electricity supplies and telephone service, ordering material not available on the island, and contracting with several local builders.

Within four weeks, through the efforts of several thousand workers, 18 wooden units – each 150 feet long, 25 feet wide, with 7-foot-wide verandahs on the long sides, on hardwood footings – were ready, with another nine under construction. Each unit, subdivided into cubicles, was twinned to another by walkways, with a sanitary block between. Work was also underway on kitchen and dining blocks, recreation and other facilities, administrative and stores buildings, police station, hospital, cottages, and residences for senior staff and for the Roman Catholic priests and nuns who would be integrally involved in working with the mainly Roman Catholic evacuees.

The PWD report notes that at the end of the seventh week, the camp was essentially ready to receive 4,000 evacuees, though some work was still underway. Then, on September 15, instructions came to prepare for an additional 5,000 evacuees. Plans were made to expand the number of buildings on the original site and accommodate the balance, some 3,000, in a second section of the camp, Camp Two, on a lower terrace, about 100 feet above the Hope River. Work commenced on this site, and on expansion of the camp hospital, at the end of September. On November 13, instructions were received to discontinue any new construction. Everything already in hand, which was most of the work planned, was completed in early January.

The total cost, according to the Colonial Office in 1941, was some £375,000. The total

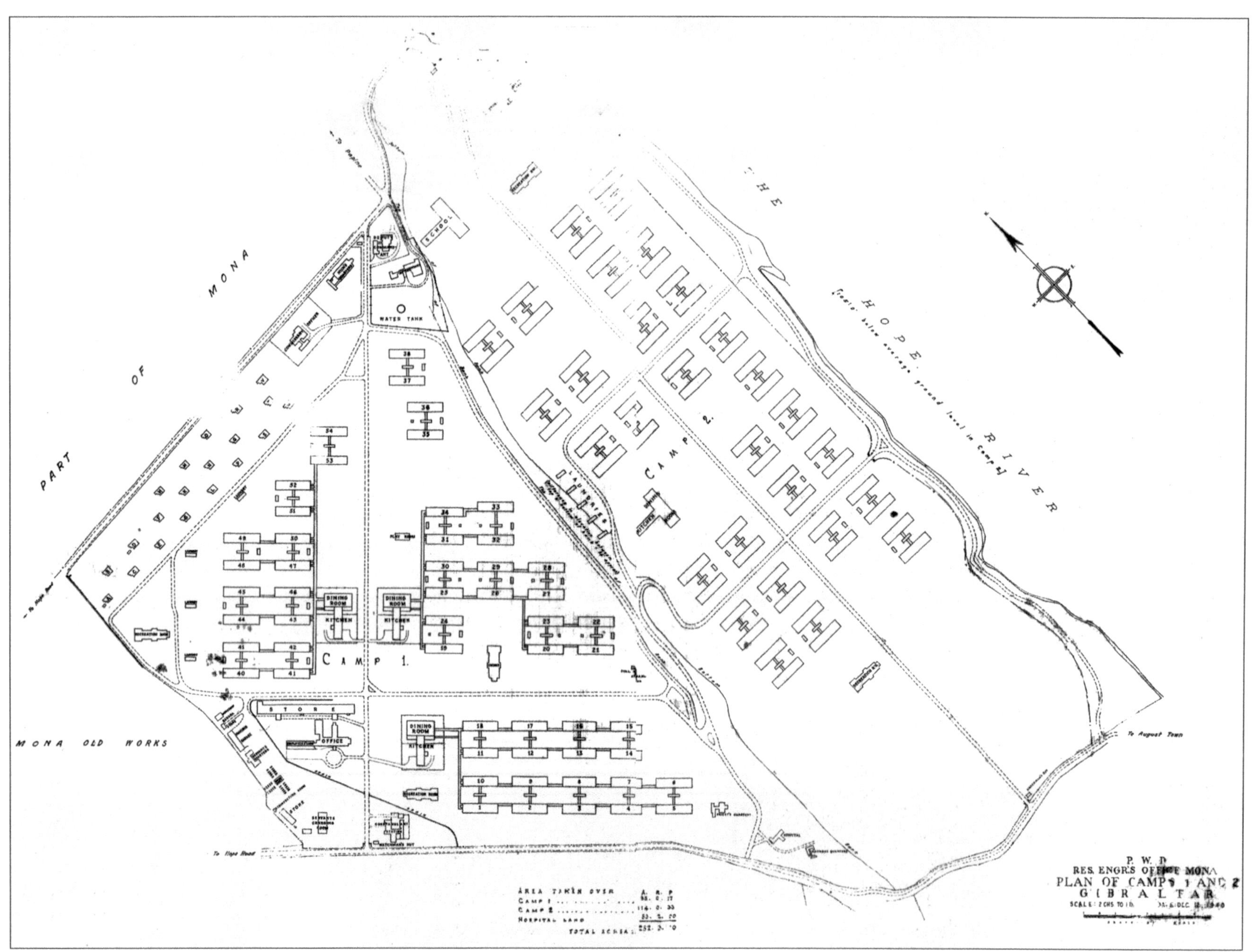

Public Works Department plan of the original (Camp One) and subsequent (Camp Two) sections of Gibraltar Camp

The two-storey Nunnery, in its later years. It was demolished in the early 1990s.

size was 252 acres: 85 acres under Camp One, 114 acres for Camp Two and 53 acres for the camp hospital.

In a 1989 newspaper article, Father William Feeney, Roman Catholic Chaplain at Gibraltar Camp, 1940–43, recalls the Catholic Church's early involvement, based on a request from the Governor and the Catholic Bishop of Gibraltar. He says that Governor of Jamaica Sir Arthur Richards visited the Jesuits in 1940, asking the local church to run the educational, religious and social aspects of the camp. Father Feeney notes that when no one religious order could spare eight religious sisters from the same community for Gibraltar Camp, without crippling ongoing work, a community was formed made up of two Franciscans, two Sisters of Mercy, two Dominicans and two Native Sisters. They moved into the Nunnery, the only two-storey building on the site, near to the Camp Commandant's quarters.

MONA SPRINGS TO LIFE AS HOME OF 9,000

Settlement Ready To Accommodate Some Population From Malta And Gibraltar.

JAMAICA'S lightning built township, Mona, which will be the haven of some 9,000 evacuees to be sent here from the imperilled war zones of Gibraltar and Malta, famous British strongholds of the Mediterranean, is now ready to accommodate at least half its future population.

A settlement for 4,000 was the first goal. The figures have recently taken a more than 100 per cent jump.

This Gleaner *report was one of several on the camp during 1940*

Jamaicans could follow preparations for the evacuees through the *Gleaner* newspaper, which had frequent reports, often alongside news from the war front. A September 21, 1940 report, with photographs of the barracks buildings, describes the new camp bounded by the Hope River on the east, August Town Road to the south, the Lindo Gap road to the north and the old Mona Estate Works to the west:

> What a change has taken place at Mona within the past two short months. The last sugar crop taken at Mona was said to be as far back as 1907 and since then a great portion of it has been in ruinate and part of it leased for raising cattle. The old aqueduct which used to bring water from the Hope River in the old sugar days is still to be seen at the west of the camp, a silent reminder of the past . . .

An October 7 report describes the area around the camp, noting that the recently asphalted road to the camp detoured off the Hope Road at Bamboo Corner, with the camp lying south-east of Papine, about a half-mile from the market. It recalls Bedward, the local prophet who tried to fly to heaven, and whose followers still lived in the area: "Their homes are mostly wattled, a few daubed with mud.

They evince little interest in the activity 'next door'. They are not particular who they have for neighbours, as long as their neighbours will have them."

The camp consisted of long rows of neat wooden huts, each with a large number from 1 to 112 painted on a short side to serve as street location. The entire compound was encircled by a wire fence, and the camp was run by a Commandant appointed by the British Colonial Office – Major Henry Simms being the first appointee. Mr E.A. Rae, formerly Deputy Mayor of Kingston, was appointed Camp Manager. Rae would be named deputy to Commandant J.L. Worlledge, who succeeded Major Simms in October 1940. In March 1941, Worlledge left for England and Rae became Acting Commandant. Also important was the Commissary Officer, who had the responsibility of finding food for the camp's population during wartime, when so much was scarce. Allan Rae recalls that meat and other perishables had been stockpiled in cold storage at Up Park Camp to ensure that there was enough for the evacuees.

The first Gibraltarians arrived aboard the slow-moving Neuralia, which had left Gibraltar on Wednesday October 9, 1940 with 1,104 passengers, 1,093 of them evacuees. They sailed with a convoy until October 13, then continued alone, trusting to prayer and to the huge red crosses painted on the ship, port and starboard. They arrived in Kingston on Friday October 24: 185 men (mostly teens and over 45s), 673 women and 246 children, evacuees from a fortress colony under 3 miles long and three-quarters of a mile wide, much of it fortress and barracks.

Thousands of Jamaicans turned out to cheer the evacuees as they rode to camp in 35-seater buses, their heavy baggage following in lorries. Volunteer priests and nuns helped lead them to their quarters from the main gate on the road to August Town, where the buses unloaded them, ahead of threatening rain; and they arrived in camp to find their beds already made, courtesy of Catholic schoolgirls anxious to make them welcome.

A second group, travelling on a Belgian ship, the *Thysville*, left Gibraltar on October 31 with 393 evacuees, arriving on November 16, at which point it was reported that there was no-one left to be evacuated; everyone left was doing military work or linked to the city council. The rest of the civilian population, some 13,000 out of a population of 22,000, had been accommodated elsewhere after months of being moved from Gibraltar to Morocco, back to Gibraltar, and eventually to Madeira (some 2,000) and war-torn Britain (around 11,000).

A plan to move the bulk of the evacuees in Britain to Jamaica was scuttled when, on October 25, the First Lord of the Admiralty advised the War Cabinet that threats to shipping from German U-boats made it impossible to transport evacuees until a new and more effective convoy system could be put in place.

The expected Maltese never came. Professor Diana Cooper of Canada's York University, in a 2001 lecture on Gibraltar Camp as a place of refuge for European Jews, said that a Maltese

SO, THIS IS JAMAICA!

CENTRE: A Gibraltar Senora and her little girlie make a charming picture framed by the porthole as they smiled with Jamaicans on the wharf on their arrival yesterday. LEFT: a scene of the disembarkation showing some of the evacuees coming down the gangway. RIGHT: piling luggage into one of the omnibuses in which the evacuees were speeded away to Camp Gibraltar Mona.

FOOD CONTROLLER NAMED DEFENDANT IN SUIT ON RICE

Mr. W. D. B. Bruce Also Coupled in Action Filed For Merchant.

The rice issue between merchants and the Food Controller reached the Law Courts yesterday when

1,100 EVACUEES NOW AT GIBRALTAR CAMP

First Batch Ended Long Voyage Yesterday

Jamaica yesterday became a haven of safety to 1,100 civilian evacuees from Gibraltar, key to the Mediterranean, the British

give over one inch of Gibraltar to the Germans," one businessman declared. "That is the spirit of the Gibraltarian. We are all

SUCCESSFUL R.A. BOMBING RAID ON ITALIAN POST

Troops Concentrations Sidi Barrani Attacked Clashes Renewed

LONDON, Oct. 25.—In Middle East the Royal Force have carried out successful raids on Italian positions

Gleaner *report on the arrival of the first Gibraltarians, October 1940*

British cartoon picked up in the local papers, September 1940

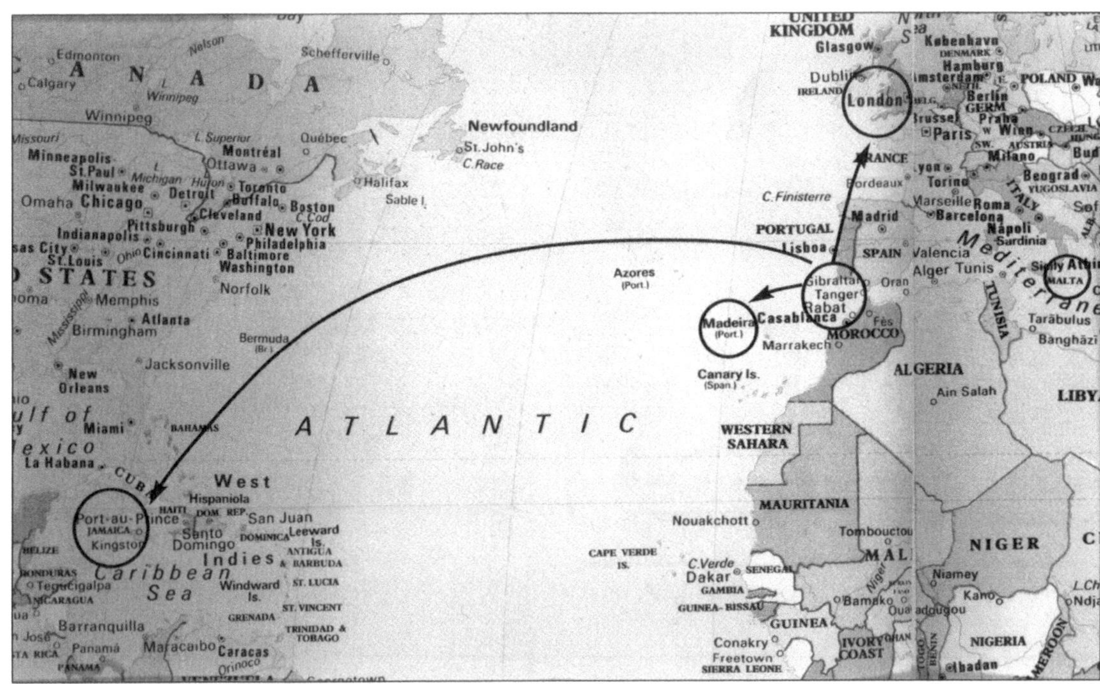

Map shows geographical relationship of Gibraltar, Malta, Britain, Madiera and Jamaica (Philips University Atlas)

Road sign recalls Gibraltar Camp

delegation visited and did not like Jamaica. In particular, they did not wish their families to be placed under the authority of black or coloured people. Father Feeney, in his 1989 *Gleaner* article, said that the civilian population of Malta refused to make the trip to Jamaica.

This left some 1,500 Gibraltarian evacuees in a facility built to accommodate 7,000.

The issue of how to most effectively use this surplus capacity was the subject of much discussion during and after 1941 among the War, Colonial and Foreign Offices and the Treasury, among others in London, and between the Colonial Office and the local administration, headed initially by Governor Sir Arthur Richards and later by Sir John Huggins. The possibility of using a section of the camp for German and Italian prisoners of war was discussed, as was the option of moving the Gibraltarians to an alternative location, and using the entire camp for prisoners of war. It was evident that there were major concerns about possible implications of having German and Italian prisoners guarded by black and coloured authorities. The provision of refuge for European Jews fleeing Hitler's policies also arose, after frantic appeals to the British government.

On February 7, 1942, a group of 153 Jewish refugees arrived in Kingston on board the *Serpa Pinto,* and were moved to Gibraltar Camp. Of this group, 147 were Polish, three were Dutch, one Belgian, one German and one American. The American, who was in charge of the group, subsequently left and the German was interned. A case of typhus on board ship led to the group being quarantined initially, after which they were subject to the same freedoms and restrictions as the Gibraltarians, including a ban on taking up employment outside the camp. Subsequently, a second group of European Jews, 107 in number, arrived in Jamaica on the *San Thome.* In 1942–43, the camp would also be temporary home to a group of Dutch refugees from the *Marques de Comillas.*

T.J. Finlayson, in *The Fortress Came First*, an extensive book on the evacuation of the Gibraltarians, notes the cancellation of a September 1942 Colonial Office plan to use Gibraltar Camp Two – the lower level – as barracks for a batallion of local militia. The plan had sparked concerns about having coloured troops in such close touch with adolescent Gibraltarian girls. Early in 1943, another proposal to house internees in the unused area was approved after the Jamaican government gave an assurance that the camps would be separated by some 200 yards.

Estimates of Expenditure for the camp prepared in December 1943 contain a file note indicating that some 186 local staff and 446 evacuee staff were employed at Gibraltar Camp, where a total of 1,530 Gibraltarian and Spanish evacuees were accommodated in Camp One; Polish and other refugees in Camp Two; and some 165 Dutch refugees in Camp Three. There were also seven Finnish internees. Allan Rae recalls his mother being given a model ship by an interned Finnish ship's captain named Oyst (the spelling is uncertain), who had made the model during his internment.

Despite the numerical designations of Camps One, Two and Three, Gibraltar Camp, as administered by Ernest Rae and his staff, seems to have operated as one institution. The Chaplain, for much of the time the Gibraltarians were in Jamaica, was Father Bill Feeney, whose brother Thomas was, at the time, head of the local Catholic community. Father Feeney and others occupied the camp's Priests' Quarters, near the top of the escarpment. The Dispensary and Matron's Quarters (later Bungalows 137, 138 and 139) were nearby.

One of the Polish refugees, a young Jewish woman named Myriam Sandzer, later writing as Miriam Stanton, recalls the camp as

> a real bustling and lively little town. We had, with the Dutch Refugees, over three thousand people living in the refugee section of Gibraltar Camp and about one thousand employees working there. We were completely self-sufficient. We had schools, a hospital, shops, offices, a police station, even a lock-up. There was always something happening, concerts, weddings, fights, scandals and unfortunately, funerals as well. We had beautiful gardens; everybody tended his own little patch.

In addition, over 100 Gibraltarian babies were born there.

Huge kitchens with their preparation areas, large wood stoves and electrically operated vegetable peelers were attached to three open-sided dining halls capable of seating 1,000 people at a sitting. Meals were served in two sittings – breakfast at 7.00 a.m. and 8.00 a.m., lunch at 12.00 noon and 1.00 p.m., and supper at 5.00 p.m. and 6.00 p.m. Cold, fresh milk was available all day. The Gibraltarians and the Jews seem to have had a say in their menus, but some people on the camp did complain about the food, and about efforts to maintain strict standards of discipline. Finlayson details an incident which caused some consternation back in Gibraltar, in which a fracas followed efforts to prevent persons taking their meals from the dining halls back to their quarters.

Entrance and exit to the camp were controlled by a Cuban-born security officer, Juan Herrera. The main gate marked on the plan – the present Post Office gate – seems to have been superseded for day-to-day use by the present Irvine Hall gate, which was closer to Papine and the scheduled tram service. Residents could come and go between 8.00 a.m. and 10.00 p.m., once they logged in and out. However, Evacuee Regulations, dated 1940 and advertised in the *Gleaner*, imposed fines on Jamaicans seeking to enter the camp without a valid pass.

A model ship given to the Camp Commandant's wife by a Finnish internee

Photograph showing the camp office: Camp Commandant Ernest Rae is standing at the desk and Catholic Chaplain Father Bill Feeney is at rear

Gibraltar Camp parade

The first sight of a wire fence, and a black man with a machete on guard, caused some fears among the Jewish refugees, some of whom are reported to have unhappy memories of Gibraltar Camp. They also charge a lack of interest among the local Jewish community, despite specific acts of kindness and welcome by individual members of that community. Some of these differences may have stemmed from distinctions between the white, European Ashkenazi Jews in the camp, few of whom spoke English, and Jamaica's Sephardic Jews. In addition, while the local Roman Catholic community had been deliberately involved in welcoming the Gibraltarians, for whom the Camp was built – including a group of about three dozen Gibraltarian Jews for whom special arrangements were made – the European Jewish refugees arrived at short notice, after a desperate appeal to the British government for refuge within the British Empire. The local Jewish community had not been briefed to expect the visitors, neither had these refugees, as a group, been briefed as to the conditions of their stay. For them, especially the many men of working age, the worst suffering stemmed from a ban on finding jobs or starting businesses outside of the camp.

Security at the Gibraltar Camp gate

Responding to a query from Lord Cranborne, Secretary of State for the Colonies, the Governor of Jamaica Sir Arthur Richards wrote on October 13, 1942, that "none of the Polish Jewish refugees who were sent to Jamaica from Portugal have at any time been interned", though restriction orders had been issued against five persons from the *Serpa Pinto* and two from the *San Thome*. The Governor continued:

> Certain Polish refugees at Gibraltar Camp have been making attempts to foster in the United States of America a propaganda campaign describing conditions in Gibraltar Camp in highly undesirable and untrue terms.
>
> Among various other misrepresentations of Jamaica now being given currency in the United States of America are references to Gibraltar Camp as a sort of "Concentration Camp", not widely different from similar institutions in Germany. There is no doubt that this campaign has been instigated by Polish Jews who have left the Camp for the United States of America, and who hope by telling harrowing and untruthful stories to persuade the United States Authorities to grant entry permits to a large number of Polish Jews now in Gibraltar Camp.
>
> In the Camp itself there is a certain feeling of unrest among the Polish Jewish section who claim that they were brought to Jamaica

under false pretences and were given to understand that they would be free to work and to live where and how they chose.

It suits these persons to allege that they are interned.

After consultation with the Chief Security Officer I am not prepared to review the arrangements under which these persons were permitted to come to Jamaica, or to consent to their accepting employment or engaging in business. In this connection I would invite reference to Lord Moyne's Secret telegram No. 957 of the 22nd of December, 1941, and to my Secret telegram No. 867 of the 26th of December, 1941. It is open to those who are not satisfied with the conditions to seek permission to enter other countries in which they consider living conditions will be more satisfactory. Those who succeed in obtaining such permission would be allowed to leave.

Stanton, in her memoir, notes that the camp had churches and a convent, and that the Jews there were given a room for a synagogue and allowed a kosher kitchen. She also recalls that the barracks rooms were each furnished with an army cot, a chair and a table. Food was plentiful, including milk, dairy products, white bread and fresh vegetables. Books, newspapers and radios were available and inmates could get day passes to leave the camp or even stay overnight with permission from the Commandant. Those refugees who had a trade were allowed to work within the camp, charging a small amount that was paid at the office, which would then pay the tailor, hairdresser, barber, shoemaker and others a wage of between 10/- and £1 each week.

Near the end of the war, Stanton says, "The Gibraltarians, all two thousand of them, left together on one big ship." In 1998, *Sunday Gleaner* columnist Hartley Neita remembered those last days:

> The women at Papine market enjoyed learning a little Spanish from the women of Gibraltar who went there on Saturdays to buy vegetables and fruits from them. And the week before they left, although it was a general secret they were returning home, somehow the women of Papine knew and hugged them, rocking from side to side, and cried their silent goodbyes.

The Gibraltarians arrived home on October 26, 1944 amid great rejoicing. On November 22, the Governor of Gibraltar sent a letter, which the *Gleaner* carried nearly two months later, expressing gratitude for Jamaica's hospitality to Gibraltarians exiled by the exigencies of war: "Now that they have returned safely to the Rock, the anxieties and discomforts inseparable from four years enforced residence in unfamiliar surroundings have been forgotten and they remember only that Jamaica gave them sanctuary and made them welcome."

Those Jewish refugees who had not already flown to Cuba and other destinations moved to the Nunnery, where they remained until they could find permanent homes.

Jamaica Patios

The evacuees also made it into popular culture. Jamaican dialect poet Louise Bennett incorporated one Jamaican reaction to the Spanish-speaking visitors in a poem titled "Jamaica Patois":

Is wha Miss Liza she dah-form,
Dah-gwan like foreigner!
Because her sister husban get
One job up a Mona!
You want hear her cut Spanish, like
She jus come out from sea!
So till dem bwoy start fe call her
De dry-lan refugee!

Gibraltar Camp

Living at Mona Camp

Until he was seven years old, Uwe Zitzow lived in internment camps in Jamaica – the last being the Mona Family Camp, established in an unused portion of Gibraltar Camp. Married internees and their families moved there around September 1943, from the Hanover Street centre (women and children) and Up Park Camp (men). Most of the residents seem to have been German and Italian professionals, construction workers and missionaries interned in West Africa early in the war. Zitzow, who now lives in Tennessee in the United States, recalls:

> I was born in Cameroon, British West Africa in May 1940, about a month before my parents and a number of other Germans were interned by the British and shipped first to Nigeria and then about six months later to Jamaica. My mother and sister and I were placed in the Women's Camp and my dad at the Men's Camp. This continued for about three years, when finally everybody was united at the new family camp in Mona. There were probably about 60 families or more. When the war was over, most of the people returned to Germany. Those who found work in other countries could go there. Some of the bachelors (who lived in the men's camp) married native women and got to stay in Jamaica. We were the last to leave the camp in 1947, living at that time just outside the camp in what used to be the officers' quarters. My dad got a job at a chocolate factory in the Dominican Republic and eventually (1952) we immigrated to the United States. I still remember quite a bit about the Mona camp (I was 7 when we left). I think it was a good life there, especially considering the alternative of living in war-torn Germany . . .

Internment Camp

In late 1943, a section of Gibraltar Camp Two, near today's Mona Rehabilitation Centre, was fenced and brought under military control for the use of German and Italian internee families previously housed apart at Up Park Camp (men) and Hanover Street (women and children). Single men stayed at Up Park Camp.

The internees were mainly professionals and tradesmen working in British West Africa when the war broke out, and later shipped to Jamaica from Sierra Leone, Gold Coast and Nigeria. The *Gleaner* noted the arrival of a large group in December 1940. German government queries about their health, via the Swiss Consul, early in 1943, evoked a spate of official correspondence. The local authorities wrote London that the internees were well cared for. However, an August 1943 letter from the Defence Security Officer to the Colonial Secretary conceded overcrowding at the female camp, adding, "the institution of the married families Camp will remove this". A November 1943 letter to the Colonial Secretary's Office from the Director of Medical Service, noted staff layoffs consequent on the transfer of women and children from Hanover Street to Mona.

Uwe Zitzow, whose father was Chief Engineer at the Ekona banana and cocoa plantation in Cameroon when the war broke out, recalls that the Mona Family Camp was a rectangle surrounded by two rows of barbed wire, with an armed guard in a raised hut at each corner. About eight barracks, each divided into several units, housed the families. Others served as dining hall and school, and one for the British staff. There was a sports field at one corner, and there were monthly movies and occasional plays or concerts, as well as trips for the children. Sunday family outings became common near the end of the war. Produce from a community garden augmented camp food supplies, and any surplus was traded to local market women. Mr Zitzow built a community oven, used to bake bread and cakes, and the family raised rabbits in their backyard.

At the end of the war, most of the internees were repatriated, though a few stayed. Some Italians skilled in construction trades established homes and businesses in Jamaica. The Vaccinos, who would supervise the laying of terrazzo flooring for the University Chapel in the late 1950s, were among them.

Military Base

The Colonial Office closed its operation and the Jamaica Battalion, previously at Palisadoes, took over the entire camp, though some huts were later occupied by government organizations such as Jamaica Social Welfare. A part of the Mona Camp was, for a time, occupied by the Ex Servicemen's Training School – until December 31, 1947 when the camp buildings, along with some 650 acres of the combined Mona and Papine estates, were handed over for a new University College of the West Indies.

It was the existence of the Gibraltar Camp barracks that allowed the new UCWI to open its doors to undergraduates in October 1948, before a single architectural plan had been drawn for the new campus.

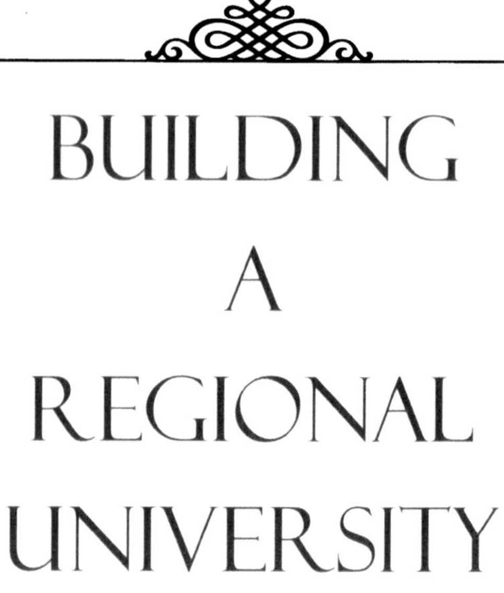

Even during the 1939–45 war, activity was underway to consider and encourage higher education in the British colonies. The Asquith Commission was established and its sub-committee on the needs of the West Indies, the Irvine Committee, recommended the establishment of a single tertiary institution for the region. The first focus was to be medicine, to fill a particular need in that area.

British academic Dr Thomas Taylor was appointed as the first Principal in late 1946, and the first office of the University College of the West Indies was opened at 62 Lady Musgrave Road in Kingston on February 1, 1947.

The Mona site was recommended from a list of several inspected by PWD official Mr R.G. Medwen, who described it as "Land south-east of Mona Reservoir and Mona Conduit, embracing all or part of Gibraltar Camp", with an approximate size of 650 acres. At a Provisional College Council meeting of January 7–9, 1948, Mr Walter Adams, Secretary of the Inter-University Council for Higher Education in the Colonies "gave as his opinion that the site was ideally situated from the point of view both of beauty and of convenience". Black and white photographs in the UWI's West Indies Collection show people on a site visit, and an early council meeting in a Gibraltar Camp building.

Following extensive negotiations with the government and the Water Commission over the land, and with the PWD and the Colonial Office over the value of the Gibraltar Camp cantonments, agreement was reached. In December 1947, the military authorities handed over the camp to the PWD, which had retained formal administrative responsibility during the military occupancy. Archival documents record that the PWD handed it on to the UCWI in March 1948.

DR. TAYLOR, HERE, TELLS OF PLANS FOR W. I. UNIVERSITY

Medical School To Be Started Oct. 1948

First step in the setting up of the new West Indies University College in Jamaica will be the creation of a Provisional Council, Dr. T. W. J. Taylor, C.B.E. D.Sc., Principal Designate of the University, told the "Gleaner" yesterday when he arrived with his wife from Britain. A Charter will have to be created, legislation or orders in council made to give the University College its powers and authority, and all the preliminary essentials should be completed in time for the first thirty medical students to be taken in by October 1948.

DR. TAYLOR

After landing from the Ariguani yesterday morning, Dr. Taylor had a busy day interviewing the Colonial Secretary, the Director of Education and others, and in the afternoon at King's House, where he and his wife are staying, he gave an interview to the Press.

"It is not too easy to be definite about this," he told reporters when asked about the exact sequence of the steps which would be taken to inaugurate the University. "What is quite definite is the Medical School. We must make every effort to have that working with the first students by the beginning of October, 1948. That is absolutely definite".

Medical School Vital

Dr. Taylor explained that this was vital because Medical Schools in Great Britain were so very full that they would not be having room not only for West Indians but for any overseas students. The supply of medically trained men must not be allowed to stop, so that by 1948, the new medical school must be started.

He confirmed that at first the medical school would be housed in temporary buildings at Camp Gibraltar, where a two-hundred bed hospital for clinical training would be provided and arrangements made for admission of about thirty students each year, or a total of about 200, since the course was six or seven

A 1946 Gleaner *story on the new UCWI*

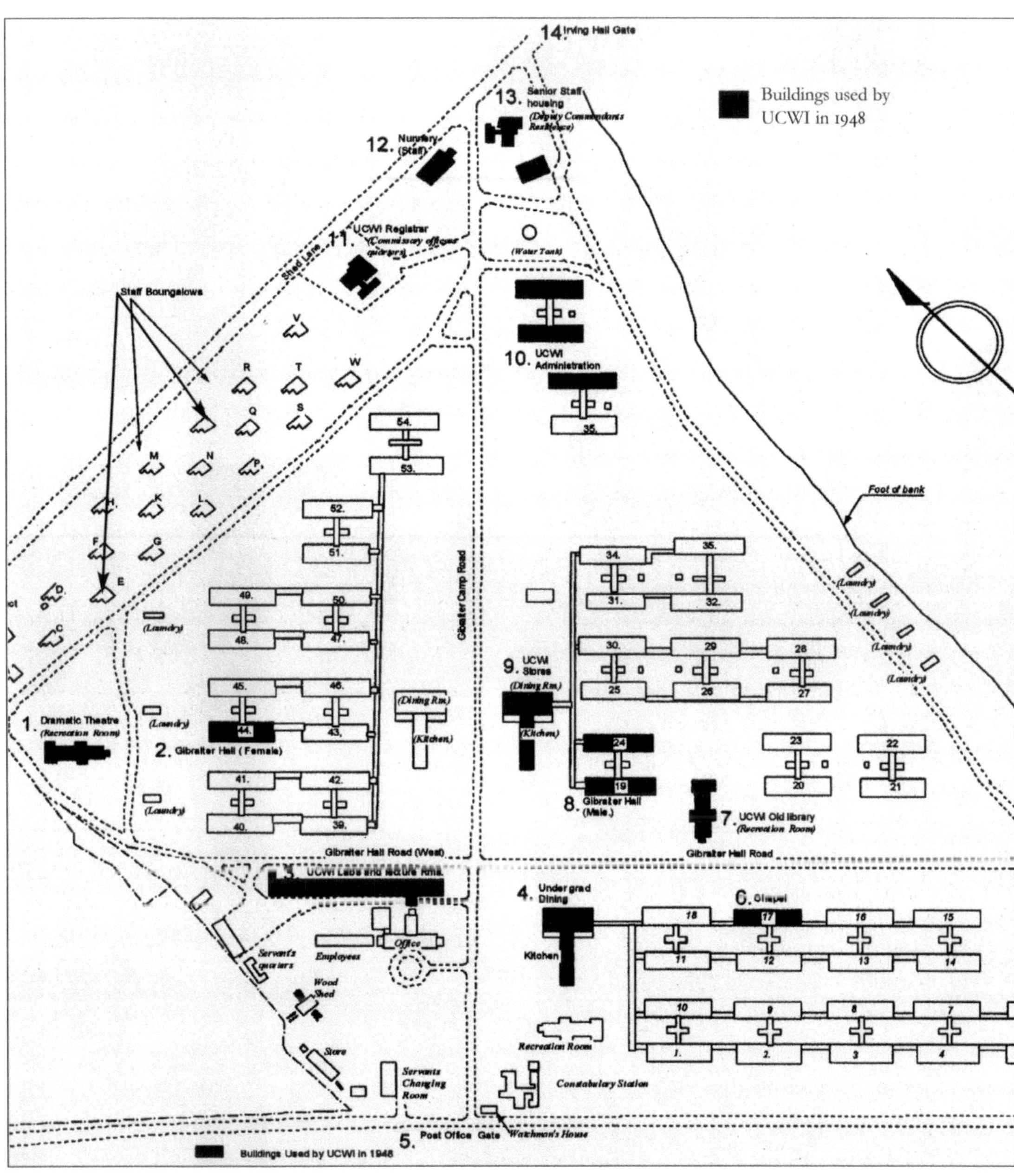

Plan of Gibraltar Camp shows buildings used by early UCWI – the Irvine Hall and Post Office gates, the Dramatic Theatre, and the Old Library provide orientation with respect to the present campus

Some of the considerations behind the transfer are noted in a 1961 history of the public water supply: "[T]he site chosen was [that] portion of the Mona Property adjacent to the reservoir compound. A block of 654 acres for the purpose was transferred to Government in 1948 in consideration of the expenditure from Imperial Funds on the construction of the Mona Reservoir."

The University College, and its adjunct University College Hospital received separate 999-year leases at a peppercorn rent of 1/- per annum; and the College bought the camp buildings at a scrap value of £12,000 – a price covered by a free grant from the colonial government.

Between the March takeover of the site and the October opening, a few huts were demolished for material to convert others into stores, laboratories, offices, classrooms, bedrooms, and dining and recreation areas.

The *Sunday Gleaner* of October 3, 1948 reported that on the following Monday at 8.00 a.m., 33 undergraduates would walk into Hut 102 of the old Mona military encampment, beginning their university careers:

> You go in through the main iron gates and there is the asphalted road leading away through an avenue of trees, the buildings in use by the University College are right and left of this road.
>
> Right, are huts 19 and 24, now the men's halls. Hut 44 at the left has been turned over to the ladies. Largish, with a through air passage, the rooms are furnished with pieces of polished yacca and mahogany, comfortable chairs and a bed, tables, dresser; for the ladies

a vanity dresser, reading lamps, a thick and colourful native straw mat on the unstained but polished floor.

Black and white photographs record the arrival and settling in of these first medical students, whose first lecture took place in a classroom at one end of the old Gibraltar Camp stores block, close to the present bus park, and was given by Chemistry Professor Cedric Hassell.

There are interior shots of the first classrooms, labs, dining hall and bedrooms, but few exteriors giving a panoramic view of the campus have survived.

The campus was essentially confined to the Gibraltar Camp area, with its entrance being the present Post Office gate from Hermitage Road. Dr Owen Minott, one of the first undergraduates, recalled it graphically during a May 2001 interview: Immediately to the left of the gate was a small Porter's Lodge, presided over by the porter, Harley, dressed in a khaki semi-uniform. Mail came and went there. Calls could be made through a rudimentary telephone exchange. Still on the left, beyond the lodge, was the long, low wooden block housing two lecture rooms at either end, as well as laboratories for Zoology (Norman Millot), Botany (Geoffrey Asprey), Chemistry (Cedric Hassell and Sydney Martin) and Physics (Francis Bowen). The Department of Anatomy was to the right of the gate, presumably in the Gibraltar Camp building designated Canteen/ Boys' Club. Next door was the Undergraduate kitchen and dining hall, one of the old Gibraltar Camp canteens, on the corner of Gibraltar Camp and Gibraltar Hall roads.

Straight up Gibraltar Camp Road, past the intersection with Gibraltar Hall Road, there was a stores building to the right (the present Personnel building), then a building used by the Extra-Mural Department. Still on the right, in what is now the Trade Union Institute/ Social Welfare Training Centre, were the offices of the Principal, Bursar and Registrar, and the UCWI Council Room. Across the road, in the apex of Gibraltar Camp Road and Shed Lane, was the Nunnery, a two-storey building used for single staff. Next door was the Registrar's House, previously the Gibraltar Camp Commissary Officer's Quarters. Anatomy Professor Walter Harper, lived in the bungalow with the tank, the old Commandant's house, which had a tennis court. The upper echelon of the maintenance staff lived in bungalows along Shed Lane. The area which became Irvine Hall was an ackee grove, and Dr Minott recalls it being bulldozed to make way for the construction.

Along Gibraltar Hall Road, going towards the escarpment, the undergraduate dining hall was to the right, in an open shed whose foundation remains. Grace was said in Latin before dinner, and woe betide anyone who was not there before the bell stopped tolling. The kitchen was immediately behind the dining hall, backing on to an internal road. The undergrads cooked there once, when kitchen staff went on strike. Across Gibraltar Hall Road from the dining room, the male undergraduates lived in Huts 19 and 24, and later in Hut 25 too. These huts ran parallel, in pairs, stretching back towards the offices. Concrete paths ran along the short ends, connecting the huts, and veran-

An undergraduate's room in Gibraltar Hall

Early UCWI students pose outside a Gibraltar Camp hut

UCWI students used one of the three Gibraltar Camp dining halls

Part of Gibraltar Camp stores block converted into the first UCWI lecture room, as noted on the sign

CABLE AND WIRELESS (WEST INDIES) LIMITED.

(INCORPORATED IN ENGLAND.)

The first line of this Telegram contains the following particulars in the order named:— Prefix Letters and Number of Message, Office of Origin, Number of Words, Date, Time handed in and Official instructions—if any.

OFFICE OF ISSUE — 29 SEP 48

Circuit.	Clerk's Name.	Time Received.	
	8	1409	5159

RK64/ ZR215/81 BARBADOS 27 29 1411 S ETATBG

= PRINCIPAL UNIVERSITY COLLEGE JAMAICA =

PLEASE ACCEPT HEARTIEST CONGRATULATIONS AND BEST WISHES FOR FUTURE OF UNIVERSITY COLLEGE MEDICAL SCHOOL ON OCCASION OF ITS OPENING =

DEVELOPMENT AND WELFARE ORGANISATION

TELEPHONED 7486 MRS. L. JOHNSON 1415

ANY ENQUIRY RESPECTING THIS TELEGRAM SHOULD BE ACCOMPANIED BY THIS FORM AND MAY BE MADE AT ANY OF THE COMPANY'S OFFICES.

Congratulatory cables arrived from several Caribbean territories

Newspaper photo shows founding father Sir Philip Sherlock (left) outside a converted Gibraltar Camp building

dahs stretched across the length of each hut on either side. Each hut was divided into 15 rooms which ran from verandah to verandah, with a half-door at either end. A shower, toilet and laundry block linked each pair of huts. A huge rock stood before the men's huts, with the words "Gib Hall" chiselled out. At one point, the men cultivated a garden. Next along the road from the men's huts was the Library, with the old Gibraltar Camp belfry and bell. A little way further along the road, on the right, Dr Minott recalls a low wooden building used as a chapel. The Old Library was used for this purpose later on, after the new UCWI Library was built. The Steward, Major Craig, lived in the old Gibraltar Camp dispensary, now the Legal Aid Clinic, while Physics Professor Francis Bowen, who was Warden of Gibraltar Hall, lived in the old Priest's House, now the Police Post. Professor Bowen grew roses and orchids. The Matron – not a medical post but the person in charge of the dining hall – may have lived in the old Matron's Quarters.

Down the escarpment, in the present Mona Bowl, a large wooden hut with two asphalt tennis courts served as gymnasium and cricket pavilion. At one time, exams were also held there. To the left of the road, in an area now covered by Preston Hall and stretching back towards the Mona Rehabilitation Centre, the old internment camp huts were mainly empty; though some were at one time used to accommodate trainee nurses, when the hospital began operating.

Along Gibraltar Hall Road West, turning left from the main Gibraltar Camp Road, the lecture rooms and labs were on the left. Further back, in a wooden bungalow on the edge of the present Senior Common Room (SCR) tennis courts, where the SCR changing facilities are now housed, was the Junior Common Room (JCR). Dr Minott recalls the ice cream kiosk run by Mr and Mrs Scott, the radiophone given by Friends of the University College, three Albert Huie paintings on the wall, and a small room that he commandeered as a photographic darkroom. The JCR was a hub on campus, where most undergraduates and staff would drop by in the evening for a chat or for entertainment.

The ten women in the first year – later joined by others – lived in Hut 44, opposite the Dramatic Theatre, close to where the Caribbean Institute of Media and Communication (CARIMAC) stands today. The Dramatic Theatre was used for plays, concerts, and, later, exams. Dr Minott also notes that five mahogany trees along Gibraltar Hall Road West, in front of the Printery, are the remnants of a set planted to commemorate the 33

A formal tea in the Junior Common Room prior to the start of the first term. The Principal (right) and Mrs Taylor (second left) entertain Governor and Mrs Kenneth Blackburn.

original UCWI students. First planted on the University's twenty-first anniversary, they were eaten by goats and replanted on the twenty-fifth anniversary.

In 1948, he recalls, the surrounding landscape included large open areas thick with Seymour grass which looked like fields of wheat in the moonlight and attracted hordes of peenie wallies when it seeded. Further back there were areas thick with fruit and other trees, including groves of ackee and mango.

The use of the Gibraltar Camp barracks was always meant to be temporary. Design of the new UCWI campus was entrusted to British architect Graham Dawbarn of the firm Norman and Dawbarn. True to the ethos of the time, the architect was a modernist; one also constrained by post-war stringencies in an institution whose initiation was being funded with colonial government funds. Dawbarn visited Jamaica and other Caribbean territories in 1947. He is quoted by a *Gleaner* columnist in February 1947 as giving the assurance that he would not develop baroque or antique buildings based on ancient traditions and suitable to other times and countries. In October 1947, in an article in the same newspaper, he writes about the paramount importance of the intangible sense of atmosphere, achieved "by a logical and sympathetic appreciation of local and current conditions; by a reasoned simplicity enhanced by local arts but married to blue skies and luxuriant vegetation".

Tenders for phase one were invited in March 1949, and in May, the UCWI contracted with Higgs and Hill Limited to erect the Library, Undergraduate Halls of Residence, Science

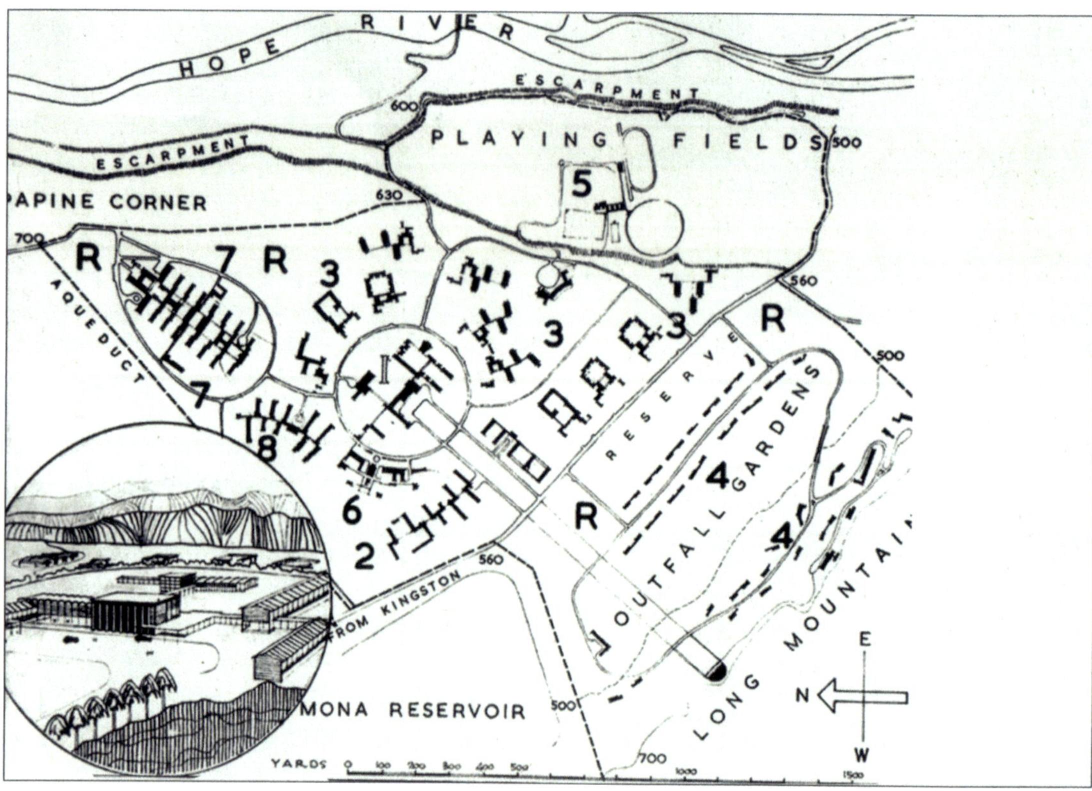

Early campus design by Norman and Dawbarn

Block (Physics, Chemistry, Zoology, Botany, Physiology, Human Anatomy, Biochemistry), as well as the Arts Block, Maintenance buildings and Science Workshop. The Hospital Board of Management made a similar contract for the building of the University College Hospital. Meanwhile, construction of staff housing was also underway as was work on the Institute of Social and Economic Research.

During festivities to install the first Chancellor – Princess Alice, Countess of Athlone – in February 1950, foundation stones were laid for the Library (by Princess Alice), the

Princess Alice at her installation as first UCWI Chancellor on February 16, 1950

The University Hospital of the West Indies, early 1950s

> Day after day, week after week from behind clumps of bushes structures peep. The continuous noise of the stone-crusher, the throbbing of the concrete mixers, and the droning of the electric saws tell a tale of ceaseless activity.
>
> The completed buildings combine beauty with comfort and utility. They present a very pleasing picture; white blocks of stone interspersed with carefully tended lawns and flower gardens . . .

A 1952 BBC Radio report also describes the noisy building site run by Resident Architect Alick Low, with some 3,500 design drawings for reference and some 1,200 men at work.

Next door, work was underway to construct the University College Hospital, which had been established under Law 40 of 1948. Originally designed by Norman and Dawbarn to hold 300 beds, this number was increased by 153 beds in 1958, to meet University of London criteria for a teaching hospital. The hospital, which was integral to the smooth operation of the University's flagship Faculty of Medicine, was declared open by Governor Sir Hugh Foot on January 15, 1953. Lady Foot formally opened the Nurses' Home on May 28, 1953.

The new college construction, Gibraltar Camp and the old sugar estate overlapped within an area bounded by the Ring Road and dubbed the "Nucleus" by the architects.

Here, the aqueduct, which sank into an underground conduit after powering the Papine sugar works, re-emerged as a prominent structure. Here too, Shed Lane, which once ran from what is now Irvine Hall gate, in a relatively straight line to Mona Road, dividing the Mona

Hospital (by the Earl of Athlone) and the first hall of residence (by Sir James Irvine, who had chaired the Irvine Committee).

Even while construction was underway, Hurricane Charlie struck in 1951 – luckily during the holidays. The wind destroyed a large wooden Gibraltar Camp structure used as the College Chapel and severely damaged several of the other original buildings.

Stage one of the new building programme deliberately stayed clear of the section of Gibraltar Camp being used by the nascent university college, Principal Taylor noting in a memo to architect Dawbarn that "the advantage of keeping building operations out of the temporary University site are very great". A sense of the atmosphere can be gathered from this 1951 newspaper report:

Arts buildings from phase one of the building programme

and Papine estates, intersected the aqueduct. This road had also come to mark the far boundary of Gibraltar Camp, bordering a series of three-room bungalows, designated A–W. These bungalows stopped just short of the Commissary Officer's residence, later home to UCWI Registrar Hugh Springer, and the Nunnery, near to the eastern end of Shed Lane. The Nunnery was across Gibraltar Camp Road from the Commandant's and Deputy Commandant's bungalows. Early aerial photographs of the Ring Road area show some of these bungalows in the lower loop of the emerging Ring Road, before they were demolished, as well as the gradual disappearance of the section of Shed Lane within and beyond the ring.

Shed Lane was discussed in early correspondence between UCWI Principal Taylor and architect Dawbarn: "It appears that the public road which runs diagonally across the site forms a division between the temporary university and the immediate building programme", a memo stated approvingly. It suggested that the section of the road that crossed the site for the new science schools could be bypassed and disused. "The remainder of the diagonal road does not interfere with any of the first three stages of the scheme and could remain as a university road until the next stages are reached."

The first phase of construction ended in 1953, although some of the buildings had been taken over from the contractors in 1951–52. The Ring Road was in place, breaching the aqueduct and cutting short Shed Lane. The buildings within the "Nucleus" were the Library, the Senate House and Registry and the Arts buildings. Outside the ring, Irvine, Taylor and Chancellor Halls spread towards the University College Hospital. Queen's Way had been cut, though the architect, Dawbarn, had originally intended it to become one leg of a two-part road divided by a wide swathe of grass and running from the Senate House, across Mona Road and up to an amphitheatre cut out on Long Mountain. The Science schools spread

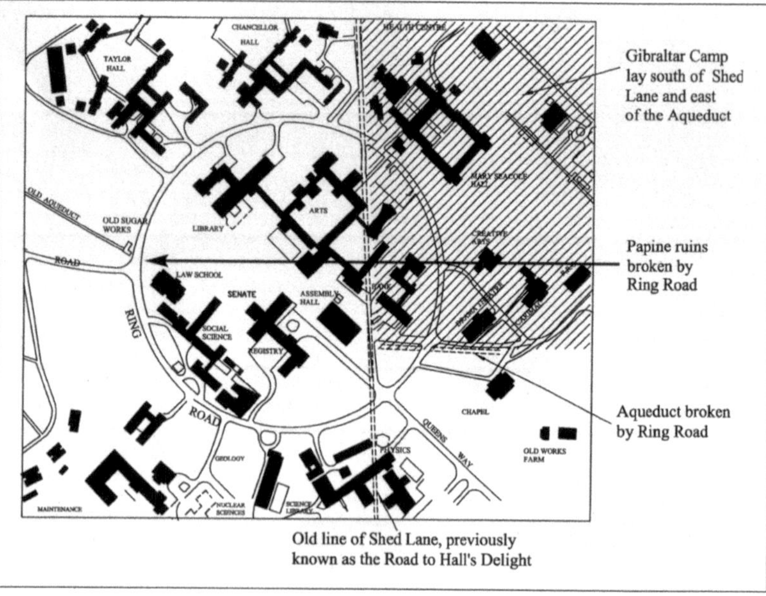

Map to show the main area where the sugar estate, Gibraltar Camp and UCWI periods overlapped

Incomplete Ring Road, showing remnants of Shed Lane and Gibraltar Camp bungalows within the "Nucleus"

Old Gib

One of the early medical students, R. Melbourne, in an article in *The Pelican* – a student annual of the 1950s and early 1960s – recalled "Old Gib":

> Each hut had its own distinguishing features. Hut 19 was quiet and dignified; Hut 24 given to spasmodic outbursts of boisterousness; Hut 25 perennially talkative, indeed the home of a certain verbose society; Hut 30 the home of genius in all its forms, for we were indeed versatile; and Hut 31 a den of unconventional brilliance, a combination of brains, noise and chaos.

out along a spine between Queen's Way and Mona Road.

The Principal's Report for 1951–52 listed the temporary huts still in use as Gibraltar Hall (male undergraduate huts), the Registry including the Bursar's and Steward's offices, the Council Chamber, the Extra-Mural Department and the Book Bindery. The temporary Science Labs were still being maintained. Funds allocated in the wake of Hurricane Charlie had, by then, enabled the campus authorities to put forward the construction of the Registry and Senate House, as well as the Students' Union and the Olympic-size swimming pool. The Senate and Registry were completed in August 1953, in time for the November visit of Queen Elizabeth II.

The SCR facilities were also being improved, first through the addition of a swimming pool and three tennis courts, and later through the replacement of the original wooden huts with a new structure.

Queen Elizabeth II visiting the UCWI in November 1953

By the mid-1950s, then, the focus of activity on the Mona site was shifting, from the Gibraltar Camp Road and its environs over to the new hub. The most unwilling to move were the men of Gibraltar Hall – the first undergraduates, who had grown accustomed to their barracks quarters and the early camaraderie amid basic amenities. Most of them moved in 1953, taking with them the old Gibraltar Camp bell, which they shook down out of its belfry during a riotous night which one participant remembers as part demonstration, part celebration. The bell broke in the process and was borne off to Chancellor Hall, to which the Gib Hall men had been assigned and where the bell would become a symbol of hall rivalry for a decade, before it disappeared off campus.

A few of the men of the original medical class managed to remain for another year. However, in June 1954, after a valedictory Gibraltar Hall tea party near to hall gardens which had been the pride and joy of future doctors Owen Minott and Ken Standard, the laggards were made to pack up and move to their new quarters.

The University College was growing, yet students from across the West Indies were still required to live on hall for most or all of their campus life, building up regional linkages at a time when Federation was still on the agenda. This regulation would go in the early 1960s, under pressure of numbers.

The period 1956–58 saw the construction of the Mary Seacole Hall and the extension of Irvine Hall; the construction of buildings in the Arts, Education and Mathematics areas; an extension to the Physics building; a new Medical Research Council ward and lab (later the Tropical Metabolism Research Unit); a new changing room for the Olympic-size swimming pool; and some new staff housing.

Women students living on Mary Seacole Hall made waves on March 8, 1960, when they picketed a ground-breaking ceremony for the Arts Lecture Theatre – later named after Professor Neville Hall – across Ring Road from their hall. The ceremony was beginning, with Princess Alice and the Princess Royal in attendance, when the formally gowned young women marched up and surrounded the site, in total silence. Some of their placards read: "Mary Seacole has walked for three years and she is tired" and "We seek it here, we seek it there – happy meals in our own atmosphere." Seacole Hall had been built without a kitchen, leaving Seacolites to walk to Irvine Hall for meals.

The late 1950s also saw the gradual disappearance of the smaller Shed Lane bungalows, which had originally been used as staff housing. The old Commandant's and Deputy Commandant's houses and the old Commissary Officer's quarters, where Sir Hugh Springer, the first UCWI Registrar, lived, continued in use for some years more. Insurance data records for 1957 note, "Old Works Farm demolished", presumably a reference to some of the old Mona Estate buildings.

A major addition to the campus landscape came in the late 1950s. The UCWI Council had agreed, from January 1952, to the provision of a non-denominational place of worship. Then, in 1955, on a visit to Gale's Valley in Trelawny, UCWI Chancellor Princess Alice saw a disused Georgian stone building dating from 1799 – part of a sugar estate belonging to Mrs Kelly Lawson. At the request of the Chancellor, who had received an anonymous personal gift to underwrite the building of a chapel, it was donated for the purpose.

So, beginning in April 1956, the University's first Resident Engineer, A.D. Scott, "painstakingly pulled down, numbered and transported to Mona the cut limestone blocks of an eighteenth-century rum-store from Hampden Estate in Trelawny", as historian Douglas Hall recorded in *The UWI: A Quinquagenary Calendar, 1948–1998.*

The decision to place the chapel on the lawn, 100 yards south-east of the Queen's Way, at the southern end of the aqueduct which served the Mona Estate, is recorded in the Principal's Report 1954–55, and details of the transformation from rum-store to chapel are captured in a bound volume by Norman and Dawbarn, in the UWI Archives. UCWI alumnus Allan Kirton, who came on campus in 1952, recalls seeing the numbered blocks piled on the lawn

Seacolites protest – painting in the Maintenance staff canteen

Stamp showing UWI Senate building

Centre: *The Gibraltar Camp church bell, later used by the UCWI, and a source of rivalry between the male undergraduate halls during the 1950s and 1960s*

The old building at Gale in Trelawny, which was reconstructed as the University Chapel

Detail from the University Chapel ceiling

At right: *The Charter of the University of the West Indies*

over many months. The first service at the Chapel was held on June 21, 1959, under the coffered ceiling bearing the Arms of the Chancellor and the Arms and Ancient Seals of all the countries contributing to the University's recurrent expenditure in 1950. The portico would be added in 1962.

The second phase of building was underway when the UCWI, until then a college of the University of London, received its own independent Charter in 1962.

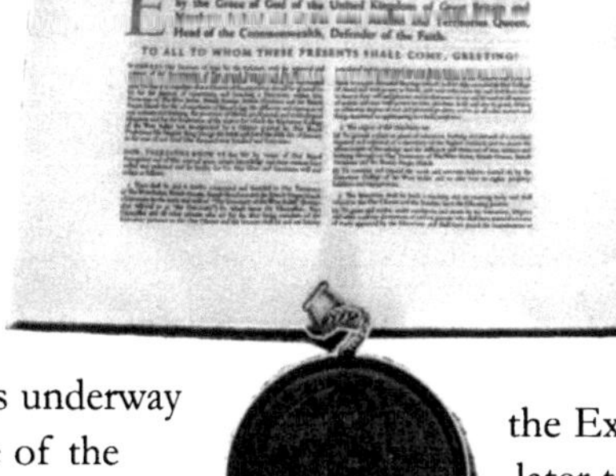

ELIZABETH THE SECOND

TO ALL TO WHOM THESE PRESENTS SHALL COME, GREETING!

Coincidentally, both Jamaica, host of the Mona campus, and Trinidad and Tobago, where the St Augustine campus had been established in 1960, became independent in 1962. The Cave Hill campus in Barbados would be established in 1963, by which time the Mona Campus had a new Assembly Hall in the nucleus, new buildings for Arts, Education, Math and Social Sciences, and a Bookshop/Soda Fountain complex. The Library had been extended and the science area had seen extensions to Physics, Chemistry, Zoology and Botany, Anatomy and Physiology, as well as new blocks for Pharmacology, Inorganic and Physical Chemistry, and a new Faculty of Medicine. Improvement or extension work had been done on some of the halls. And, along Gibraltar Camp Road, a new building for the Sub-Department of Social and Preventive Medicine had been put up, replacing one of two dining room and kitchen blocks which had faced each other across the road during the Gibraltar Camp period. Part of the other was retained and would house the Law School and, later, the UWI Personnel Department. Further up the road, towards the Irvine Hall gate, there was a new University Health Centre facing a Social Welfare Centre put up by the Jamaican government as part of the Extra-Mural Department – later to become the School of Continuing Studies. Other Extra-Mural Department developments

Gibraltar Camp laundry cisterns in front of CARIMAC

underway included a Trade Union Education Institute and a Radio Education Unit. Elsewhere on the campus the SCR was in new premises behind the chapel gardens, adjacent to the old Mona Works. A Stores and Maintenance Services building had been erected and new housing had been built.

Gradually, most of the remaining Gibraltar Camp structures disappeared, including the huts between the present printery and Mary Seacole Hall. The Creative Arts Centre – now the Sir Philip Sherlock Centre for the Creative Arts – was opened in 1968 and nearby, in 1978, a home for CARIMAC, which retains a stand of Gibraltar Camp laundry cisterns on its front lawn. Other new buildings on the campus during the 1970s were the Computer Centre, and the Norman Manley Law School.

The 1980s saw the start of a new building thrust, with external grant and soft loan assistance. Highlights included the Child Development and Training Centre near the August Town gate, the Biotechnology Centre, the UWIDITE building and a new postgraduate housing scheme. But the end of the decade also saw devastation of the campus environment, when Hurricane Gilbert struck Jamaica in 1988. Many buildings were damaged. Some roofs lifted, taking papers, books and equipment along. Some older buildings, the Nunnery included, were badly affected. And many of the older trees, which had offered shade and brightened the view of many thousands of students across the years, were broken and scattered.

Reconstruction in the wake of Gilbert would merge with planned additions during the early and mid-1990s. This period brought major extensions to the Library and Health Centre, new and expanded facilities for the Natural and Life Sciences, new buildings for Education, a new Social Science lecture theatre, buildings for Computer Science, Gender Studies, Environment and Development, Nursing Education, and the Centre for Nuclear Science. The A.Z. Preston housing complex – which spread across the escarpment behind the Students' Union, covering much of the

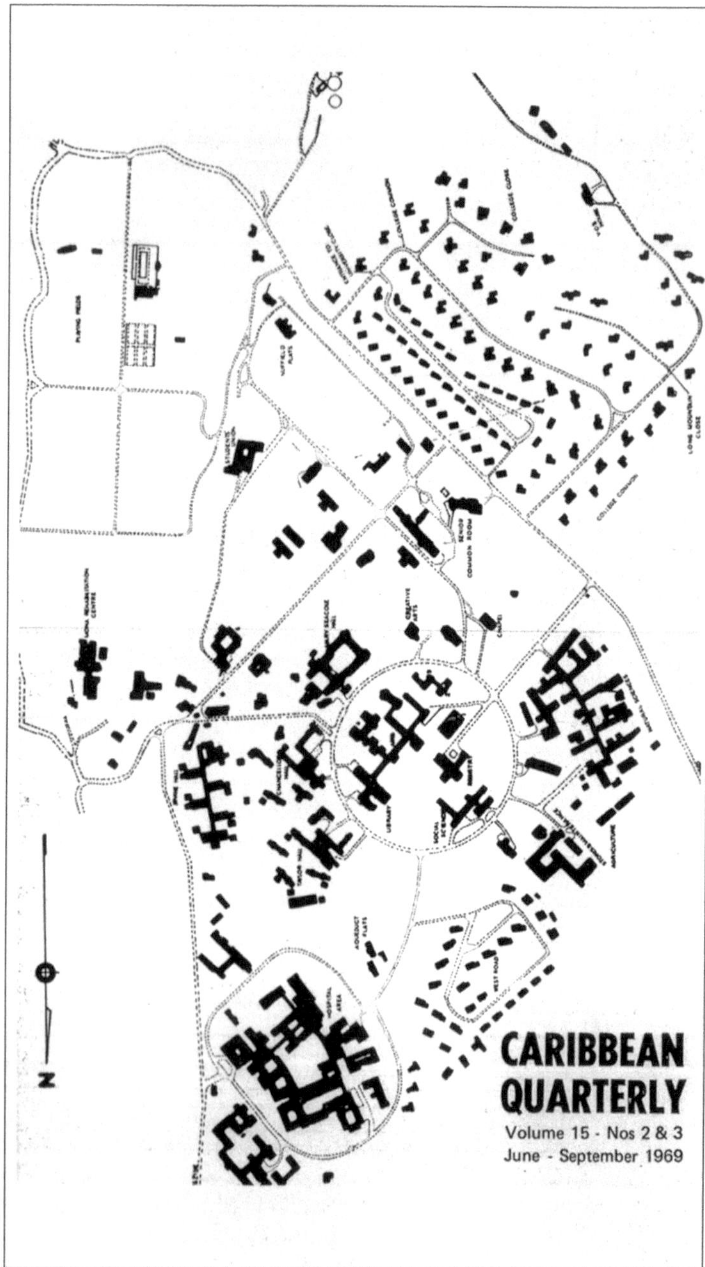

1969 plan of the UWI campus

Old Gibraltar Camp stores block, later used as UCWI labs and lecture rooms

Mona Police Station

area once used for internees at Gibraltar Camp – was opened in 1995. In the computing arena, the campus also developed a major fibre-optic backbone for its first local area network (LAN).

The 1990s also saw the demolition of the two-storey Nunnery – which housed nuns and then refugees during the Gibraltar Camp period – and the Commissary Officer's bungalow, which was later the Registrar's residence: "green lattice work and jalousies, shingled roof, airy rooms", History Professor Patrick Bryan recalled in an interview. The History Department argued unsuccessfully for the UWI to retain the Nunnery, Registrar's house and Bungalows 1 and 2 as authentic units representative of the Gibraltar Camp period.

The original stores building, which was converted into the first UCWI lecture rooms and laboratories, was later used as offices, classrooms and stores, and eventually allowed to deteriorate. The historic first classroom, for which restoration efforts had been mooted but not successfully pursued, was pulled down in summer 2001, with the rest of the stores block following in January 2002.

Two of the large recreation halls from the Gibraltar Camp period – the Dramatic Theatre and the Old Library – have continued in use, mainly as examination halls. The Animal House, near the Post Office gate, was originally part of an old Gibraltar Camp kitchen/dining hall, later used by the first UCWI undergraduates; the Personnel Office still uses a part of another original kitchen/dining hall, earlier used as a store by the UCWI authorities. The Commandant's and Deputy Commandant's bungalows at the top of Gibraltar Camp Road remain in place, as do the three bungalows near the escarpment above Mona Bowl, although the original Priest's House is virtually unrecognizable under the police station.

The development of the University's physical structures has interfered less with the old sugar estate remnants, since the imposition of the Ring Road and "Nucleus" over the Papine Works ruins and the aqueduct, and the atrophying of Shed Lane in the 1950s. An early decision to develop a green space around the Mona Works ruins, was undoubtedly a factor in their having remained relatively undisturbed. In 2001, however, the University elected to develop two of the major ruins – the old distillery and rum store on the lawns of the SCR Hotel (renamed the Mona Visitors' Lodge) and the boiling house/curing house complex. The old distillery, whose foundation and some archways had remained solid, has been re-floored and marketed as a reception area and events venue. The boiling house/curing house complex is planned to become an upscale restaurant and bar. Building excavation close to the ruins recently stumbled on old bricks and the remains of an iron cauldron which hark back to the sugar estate period and which seem to beg for rescue archaeology.

The focus of UWI is now through the main gate, up Queen's Way to the Assembly Hall and Senate building, with the Chapel on the right and the aqueduct, a symbol of the past, stretching across the lawns and unifying the old Papine and Mona estates. Clockwise from Queen's Way, there are sectors occupied by the Natural and Life Sciences, Medical Research, Social Sciences and Law, Arts and Education – including Communication. Student housing stretches from the aqueduct, east to the escarpment and down across the back of the Mona Bowl. A massive expansion of student housing, Rex Nettleford Hall, was completed in 2002.

Sir Philip Sherlock, who was involved integrally with the University from its inception, and Professor Rex Nettleford, the first graduate to be named Vice Chancellor, wrote *The University of the West Indies: A Caribbean Response to the Challenge of Change* in 1990. They suggest that "Mona, once a place of suffering and misery for earlier generations of Jamaicans, became a symbol of West Indian unity and nationhood, and buildings erected to serve the purposes of war cradled the University of the West Indies".

Conclusion

The Mona campus of the UWI encapsulates a rich store of recorded past experience, events and artefacts spanning hundreds of years. These include the inferred legacies of the Tainos and the Spanish; the documentary records and architectural remnants left by the English plantation owners; the labour input of the African slaves and East Indian indentured workers; the river flow captured in the aqueduct and coveted by the water authorities; the barracks occupied by the Gibraltarian evacuees, the Jewish refugees and the interned Germans and Italians; the army camp; and the regional university. Yet much has also been lost over time. Due care and a relevant heritage policy can help ensure that the drive to provide facilities within which to pursue educational goals, will not further threaten remnants of this rich heritage.

With respect for the past as well as a vision for the future, the UWI can conserve, analyse and interpret its rich historical store. At Mona, the past is always present.

Memories of Mona

Early lecturer R.B. Le Page recalled his UCWI years in *Ivory Towers: The Memoirs of a Pidgin Fancier:*

> All the teaching and laboratories were housed to begin with in Gibraltar Camp, a wooden hutted camp which had housed wartime refugees . . . The site was truly magnificent: a sloping disc of tough grass, mango trees, Royal Palms and coconut palms a mile in circumference between the Botanic Gardens at Hope and the foot of Long Mountain, on the far side of which lay Kingston Harbour enclosed by the Palisadoes, the airport at Port Royal and the Caribbean Sea. The huge and lovely masses of the Blue Mountains formed our northern backdrop, over the ridges of which the white cloud cascaded as the day progressed towards the teatime showers of rain. Cows, goats and donkeys grazed along the huts, and one's lectures were punctuated by bovine flatulence, the sound of mangoes being pulled from the trees by the cows' long tongues, or passionate, dispairing hee-haws. These often seemed like a commentary on one's prize aphorisms.

VIEWING CAMPUS HISTORIC FEATURES

Remnants of Sugar's Heyday

The aqueduct provided the water that irrigated the fields and turned the mills of both the Papine and Mona sugar estates, as well as those at nearby Hope and Ripleys. It is therefore appropriate to begin any tour of the sugar estate ruins and remnants on the Mona campus near to the boundary with the University Hospital, where the aqueduct begins its southward trek. The reservoir, which used to feed the aqueduct, was itself fed from the neighbouring Hope Estate system, whose water was drawn from an inlet built into the bank of the Hope River. This dam was filled in and became part of the foundation when the University Hospital was built in the early 1950s.

This first section of aqueduct on the UWI property starts out solid. It then rises into the air, reaching up to 12 feet, the variation in height compensating for changes in the slope of the land, as well as gradually raising the water to the height necessary to turn the Papine wheel and attached mill. The gradual rise may even create the illusion that the aqueduct slopes upwards as it progresses across the Papine Estate.

The aqueduct's arches were constructed in two sizes – the first ten with a span of 66 bricks, giving an arch 10 feet or just over 3 metres wide; the next five arches having a span of 91 bricks, giving an arch 14.25 feet or nearly 4.5 metres wide.

About half-way between the hospital boundary and the Ring Road, the outline of a tank can still be seen on the Aqueduct Road side of the aqueduct. It no doubt provided water for humans, livestock and plants.

The Papine slave village appears to have been located between an internal estate road, in the area of the present boundary with the

The aqueduct

hospital, and the tank. Two survey maps show "Negro Houses and Gardens" clustered on both sides of the aqueduct, with more apparently on the present Taylor Hall side. The overseer's house appears to have been sited in what is now the West Road area. The Papine Great House, of which nothing remains, is shown on old survey maps as having been located along an estate road which ran from Shed Lane, up to the works and then parallel to Shed Lane for a distance of some 22 chains. The house and its gardens were set on 10 acres of land. Estimates as to its location range from behind Taylor or Irvine Halls, to the front of the United Theological College of the West Indies, across the Papine Road from the UWI campus.

Close to the fence around Taylor Hall, there is also a tomb from a later period. It marks the remains of Jaghi, who died in 1929 aged 42 years. From his name, Jaghi was an East Indian, one of many who lived and worked in the area; perhaps from the "Coolie Village" said to have been located on the site of the present Irvine Hall.

Past the slave village, the aqueduct ran into the top of the Papine wheel-house, which housed the massive overshot water-wheel, used to turn the mill next door. The walls of the water-wheel housing remain intact. The neighbouring mill-house, with its inclined earth slope for bringing in the canes, is a ruin. The wheel-house and mill house are in the corner of the present Aqueduct and Ring roads.

Across the Ring Road, a few bits of brick wall are all that remain of the rest of the Papine Works complex. This would have included a boiling and curing house, where the

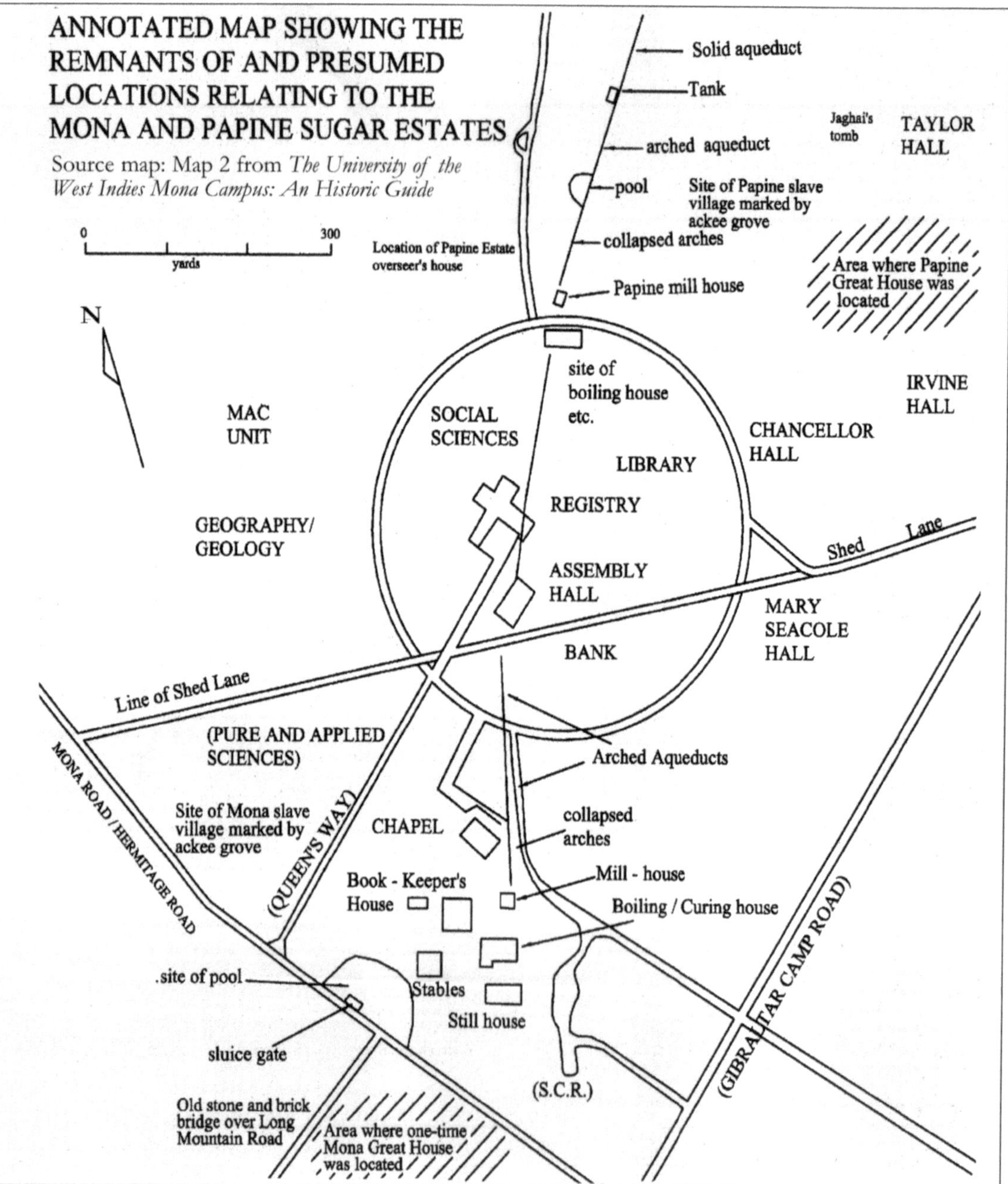

Map of ruins from the sugar estate period

Tank at side of aqueduct, near Aqueduct Road

Run-off channel in the aqueduct

Chapel and gardens

sugar cane juice from the mill was slowly turned into sugar; and a distillery or still-house for making rum.

After turning the Papine wheel, the water from the aqueduct sank into a cistern, re-emerging close to Shed Lane. Its path would have led past the Norman Manley Law School, past the eastern end of the Senate building and Registry, and under the Assembly Hall. The aqueduct can be seen again east of the Assembly Hall, close to the bank and book-shop building. In this same vicinity, a small stretch of road leads from Queen's Way towards the bank. If you were to follow the line of that road eastward, it would lead you straight up Shed Lane, the remains of which now run only from the Ring Road to the Irvine Hall gate, between Mary Seacole and Chancellor Halls. This road once ran right across the campus, connecting to the Mona Road near the present-day Mona Reservoir and thence to Kingston, and separating the Papine and Mona estates, with the Papine Estate entry being on this road. The main entrance to the Mona Estate seems to have been on what is now Hermitage Road.

Past the bank, the aqueduct is broken by the Ring Road, but it then cuts a stone swathe across the lawn to collapse behind the Chapel – a relic of the old sugar estate period, but from Trelawny not St Andrew, re-erected on the UCWI site between 1956 and 1959. The Chapel Garden abuts the Oriental Garden which frames the old Mona sugar estate ruins.

The tomb of A.Z. Preston, UWI Vice-Chancellor from 1974 until his death in 1986, is located in the Chapel Garden, as are urns containing the ashes of Sir Philip Sherlock and his widow, Lady Sherlock. Sir Philip, who died in late 2000, served with the Irvine Committee which recommended establishing the UCWI, and then worked with the University from its inception.

In times past, the aqueduct would have run right up to the wall of the wheel-house, pouring water over the top of the overshot wheel and turning it by sheer weight. The wheel would then have turned a spindle, attached to rollers which pressed the juice out of the cane fed into the mill from carts drawn up the inclined earth slope. The mill house, next to the water-wheel housing, is a ruin.

From the mill house, the cane juice would have flowed through a wooden trough – long since rotted – into the boiling house where it was led through a series of cauldrons, fired no doubt by bagasse trash, until the juice crystallized into wet sugar. The attached curing house, largely intact but for its roof, is where the wet sugar would have been set to drain, before being packed in hogsheads, loaded in wagons and drawn to the Port of Kingston for shipment to England.

Mona wheel housing

These two linked buildings are scheduled for conversion into a restaurant, which is to retain as much of the original building as possible.

Some, or sometimes most, of the crop would have been converted into rum in the still-house or distillery, located south of the boiling and curing house. The distillery, which had a water tank at the west of the building and furnaces set in the southern and western walls, was built in 1759 – the date carved in one of the arches of the ruined building. A small, strongly built room at the southern end was used as a rum store, where the liquour was kept to mature in puncheons until ready for sale. The still-house ruins have been cleaned and paved for use as a reception facility and stage.

Two functionaries, the overseer and the bookkeeper, had houses in the Mona Works area. A foundation, with steps, may mark the ruins of the overseer's house, which would have been in view of both the works and the slave village near the Queen's Way gate. The slaves would have generated the grove of ackee trees, a few of which remain scattered through the Chemistry Department parking lot. The bookkeeper's house, the only sugar estate building from either estate to have survived intact, is located behind the Chapel, and now houses the Archaeology Laboratory.

Other ruins in the area include a tank or trough, and some standing pillars, presently covered and used as a plant nursery, believed to be the remains of the stables.

The water from the aqueduct would have spilled from the Mona wheel and been led away into a pond, with a brick sluice gate whose remnants remain on the side of the Hermitage Road, between the main and post office gates.

Across the road, in what is now College Common, should lie the remains of an early Mona Great House and outhouses, shown on eighteenth-century survey maps. To date, the site has not been located.

Still inside College Common, a sturdy brick and cut-stone bridge spans the August Town Gully, on Long Mountain Road, beside a newer concrete culvert. The road would have led up Long Mountain where the Mona Estate slaves had their provision grounds, and the bridge may have been built to facilitate the movement of carts dumping cane trash.

By the end of the eighteenth century, the Mona Estate house appears to have been moved to the location of the present Mona Great House, on a hillside looking across the Mona Road. This present great house, built on an earlier foundation, is shown on an 1831 map, when the Mona Estate was still in the hands of the heirs to William and Thomas Bond. After Independence in 1962, it is said to have been considered as a possible official residence for the Jamaican prime minister, based on attractiveness, location and the symbolism of a former slave master's home becoming home to the children of slaves. The Mona Great House lies outside of the UWI Mona property.

The Mona Estate bookkeeper's cottage, now the Archaeology Lab

Mona still-house ruins

Boiling/curing house ruins

1. Deputy Commandant's house and Commandant's house with tank
2. Old laundry cisterns
3. Dramatic Theatre, formerly a Gibraltar Camp recreation hall
4. Stores block – later, first UCWI labs and lecture rooms; demolished 1990s–2002
5. One of three Gibraltar Camp kitchen/dining halls; adjacent was a Boys' Club
6. Adjacent cottages: from top, Priest's House, Dispensary, Matron's House
7. UCWI Library was Gibraltar Camp's Sacred Heart church

Remnants of Gibraltar Camp

Recalling Gibraltar Camp

Gibraltar Camp seems to have had two entrances: the main gate on the road to August Town and the busier, day-to-day entry closer to Papine. The road was asphalted and the entire camp was fenced. It was, after all, wartime, and these were evacuees – and later refugees – for whom the local authorities had a responsibility. The internment camp, which came on stream in late 1943, three years after the Gibraltarians arrived, would have been over the escarpment, out of sight from most of the main camp.

It takes a lot of imagination to visualize Gibraltar Camp now, since so little remains. On entering the camp at the present Post Office gate, wooden, one-storey buildings, mounted on hardwood posts, were seen, symmetrically laid out. Two old buildings remain on the right hand side of Gibraltar Camp Road. One was a boys' club, and the other is what remains of one large dining room and kitchen. On the left, there was a circular drive in front of the administrative office. Behind that was a stores building the length of the entire block, which would later be converted into classrooms and laboratories for the nascent UCWI.

Turning left on Gibraltar Hall Road West, there were rows of barracks huts stretching away on the right, and then a series of laundry huts, from which a concrete cistern remains on the front lawn of CARIMAC.

Across the road, a large wooden hall, signposted the Dramatic Theatre, is one of two remaining recreation halls from that period. Both the Dramatic Theatre and the Old Library,

The old Gibraltar Camp bungalow which housed the matron

on Gibraltar Hall Road East, are used as examination centres by the UWI. The Dramatic Theatre marked the western extent of the camp.

The internal road now turned north towards Shed Lane, then right in front of a row of bungalows which backed onto the lane; a remnant of which now runs from Queen's Way as it enters the Ring Road nucleus, to a small parking lot near the bank. The three-room bungalows along this stretch had been built to house small families of evacuees, but were not allocated because of concern that there would be charges of favouritism. This row of bungalows ended near the northern end of the camp, in an apex where the Commissary Officer's Quarters, the two-storey Nunnery, the Commandant's and Deputy Commandant's houses were all located. The Deputy Commandant's house remains beside the Irvine Hall gate. The Commandant's house, next door, is part of the present Institute of Education, close to the 131,000-gallon steel tank, supplied by a main from the Hope system, which served the camp.

Walking back down Gibraltar Camp Road towards the gate, there would have been barracks on both sides, many with little gardens in front and each pair with their long verandahs back and front, joined through a shorter, narrower bathroom block. About three-quarters of the way to the crossroads of Gibraltar Camp and Gibraltar Hall Roads, there were kitchen/dining rooms on either side of the road, the dining areas with open sides. The UWI Personnel Office, on the left is located in part of one such unit; and the Social and Preventive Medicine Department on your right is built on the foundations of another.

Turning left at the crossroads, the Old Library, to your left, was the Catholic Church of the Sacred Heart. A belfry held the camp bell.

Buildings would have filled in large areas on both sides of the road, where there are presently open spaces. At the end of that road, the police station has taken over and largely obliterated the old Priest's House. Along a small side road overlooking the escarpment, is the old Dispensary, now the Law School's Legal Aid Clinic while next door is the old Matron's House, now an annex of the UWI's Archaeology Lab. And, within the Preston Hall compound, a set of concrete cisterns from another laundry area on top of the escarpment, has been retained.

Nothing remains of the old internment camp which once occupied a part of the camp built below the escarpment, close to the present Mona Rehabilitation Centre, where a number of German and Italian families were kept under army supervision for part of the war.

Old recreation hall – now the Dramatic Theatre

Gibraltar Camp Commandant's house and camp water tank

Remains of an old dining hall and kitchen – now the UWI Personnel Office

The old Sacred Heart church, now the Old Library

Mona Buildings

Sherlock and Nettleford, in their 1990 look at the UWI, recall the development of the Mona and St Augustine campuses thus:

> The extensive building programme was free from examples of monumentitis, a form of physical over-expansion accompanied by severe functional anaemia . . . The tendency was toward austerity.

Early medical students, looking back, have a somewhat different perspective, as stated in *UWI: A Photographic Journey*:

> While few of the early buildings were architecturally inspiring, their setting certainly was. The aqueduct which had carried water from the Hope River to the sugar works had survived remarkably well, and enough of it was retained (perhaps more should have been) to both frame the campus and provide visual links with the past . . . The early buildings were carefully conceived to cater to the needs of the tropics. It is debatable how successful they were. The main hospital wards, with their wide, open balconies were among the most successful. In the era of Sir Arthur Lewis the need for expansion under economic constraints led to continuing economies in building. But several buildings in the sixties and seventies were more creative – the Geology building, the Creative Arts Centre, the Psychiatry building and the Norman Manley Law School building, for example.

Tracing the Roots of the UWI

The first 33 students entered the University College of the West Indies through an iron gate, from the Hermitage Road – what is now called the Post Office gate. Their environment was made up of remnants of Gibraltar Camp, including several buildings not then in use, which were later demolished. Their classes took place in the long block of labs and lecture rooms divided out of the old Gibraltar Camp stores building, which the UWI finished demolishing in January 2002.

Left along Gibraltar Hall West, the female undergraduates lived in Hut 44, in front of the present CARIMAC building, near to the old recreation hall which would be used for stage productions and as an exam hall. Right, along Gibraltar Hall East, the men lived in Huts 19 and 24, between the present Personnel building – then used for Stores – and the old UCWI Library.

Further along that road, the three cottages on the escarpment – the present Police Post, Legal Aid Clinic and Archaeology Lab annex – were used for staff housing, as were the old Commandant's and Deputy Commandant's houses which remain near Irvine Hall gate, and the Commissary Officer's Quarters, the Nunnery, and some of the small cottages along Shed Lane – all now demolished. Some of the empty barracks were used, for a while, as studios for Jamaican artists, according to the recollection of artist and educator Jerry Craig, whose father Major Karl Craig was the UCWI's first Steward. Craig recalls that Sir Philip Sherlock, who assisted the Irvine Committee

Mahogany trees planted to commemorate the first undergraduates

and was involved with the University from its inception, arranged for this while he was Vice-Principal of Mona and head of the Extra-Mural Department.

To commemorate the first medical students – 23 men and 10 women from across the region – the alumni planted 33 mahogany trees along Gibraltar Hall Road. Five remain, in front of the UWI Printery.

As the campus developed during the early 1950s and beyond, the focus shifted. Shed Lane, running from the Irvine Hall gate, now ended at the Ring Road, except for a small section retained as a slip road within the "Nucleus". Inside the Ring Road, the low zigzag of the old Arts block with its cut-stone end wall, the Senate building and the Assembly Hall are among the original buildings, designed by British modernist architects Norman and Dawbarn. The original Science blocks, the first four halls of residence and the Students' Union, near the escarpment, were others. A new main entrance had been created, and a road called the Queen's Way ran from the entrance to the Senate building in the centre of the Ring Road complex.

Public Art and Special Collections

Public artwork and special research collections complement the modern as well as the historic elements of the UWI Mona campus. In many instances, their importance reaches beyond the UWI community.

Chapel Art: The University Chapel, a Jamaica Georgian building whose 1799 construction date is carved into the stonework outside, was reconstructed in the late 1950s as a symbol of regional spirit. Its pews are made of mahogany from Belize (then British Honduras); while the flooring for the steps which mount to the gallery is constructed of greenheart from Guyana then British Guiana. The font is of Barbadian coral limestone, which was carved with ackee and breadfruit motifs by Karl Broodhagen. The lectern, in the form of the pelican which is part of the UWI's crest, was carved by Jamaican sculptor Alvin Marriott. It was Marriott who also carved, in relief on wood, the arms and ancient seals, which are the highlights of the coffered ceiling. The East

Chapel window

Window, a gift of Princess Alice, was designed by Mr E. Liddall Armitage of the Whitefriars Stained Glass Studios of London. Besides the risen Christ and the Virgin Mary, it pictures the four evangelists, Matthew, Mark, Luke and John, as well as James, Catherine, Andrew, Anne, Thomas and Elizabeth – saints whose names are used for parishes and vestries in many Caribbean territories. St Mona is included in honour of the University. Each saint has appropriate symbols.

Conversion of Trelawny Estate distillery and rum store into the Mona Chapel

Design

Consultant architects – Norman and Dawbarn (UK)
Resident architect – Alick Low

Construction

A.D. Scott Ltd.

Subcontractors

Metalwork – Bailey & Reynolds/Kingston Industrial Works
Interior woodwork, furnishings, panelling – M. Lister
Electrical work – Bicknell & Silvera
Flooring – marble terrazzo tiles by La Cubana Tile Factory – supervised by the Vaccinos, an Italian family that originally came to Gibraltar Camp as internees during the war.

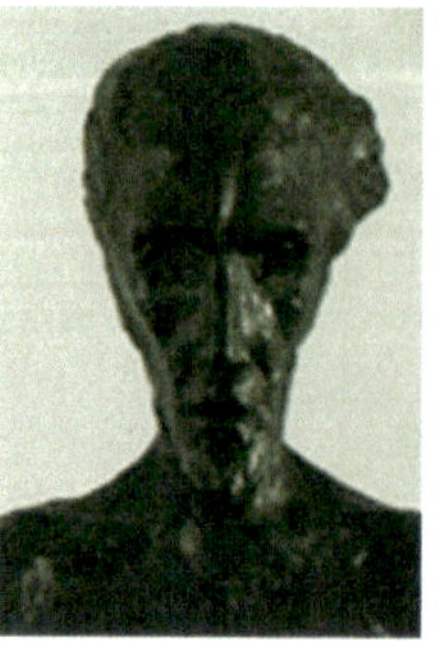

Detail of Gonzalez's Sorrowing Christ

Broodhagen font

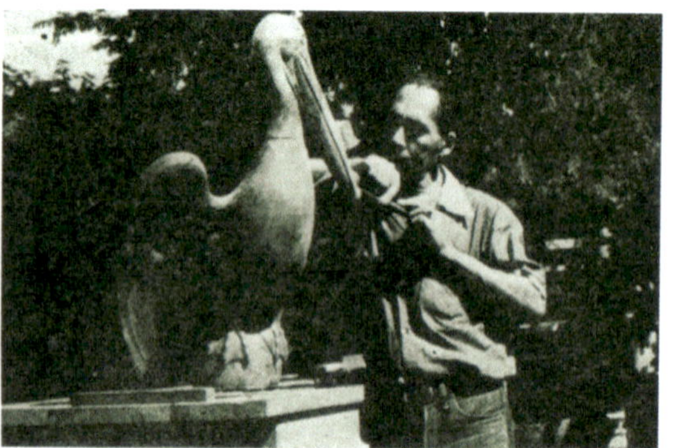

Sculptor Alvin Marriott at work on the Chapel lectern

Inside the University Chapel

The Year of the Child *mural on the side of the Assembly Hall*

The CARIMAC mural

The Good Samaritan *mural*

The arms of all the territories which were contributing members of the University College of the West Indies when the Chapel was completed in 1959, as well as those of H.R.H. Princess Alice, Countess of Athlone, then Chancellor of the UCWI and of the Earl of Athlone, her husband, are all represented on the ceiling which was painted by Leslie's Art Service. Other artistic features of the Chapel include a black concrete and steel statue of *The Sorrowing Christ* by Christopher Gonzalez, and a painting of *The Master* by Jamaican artist Ralph Campbell.

Murals: The University has two massive exterior wall murals. The first to greet persons entering the campus through the Queen's Way gate, measures 13 by 25 metres and fills the side of the Assembly Hall. It commemorates the International Year of the Child, celebrated in 1979, as well as representing activities of the then eight faculties of the UWI. The other, earlier, mural completed in 1979, is a whimsical exploration of mainly non-technological aspects of communication. It graces the side of CARIMAC. Both murals were designed by Belgian artist Claude Rahir and executed by Rahir with Jamaica School of Art students Doreen Kong and Robert Ramsay. The murals were repainted by the artist in late 1996, with the assistance of School of Art students Gaylan Robertson and Christopher Drummond.

A mural done by a former director of the Tropical Metabolism Research Unit, Angela Waterlow, depicts the tale of the Good Samaritan, with a modern cast. The mural is located on a wall of the Faculty of Medical Sciences, on the grounds of the University Hospital. Another Waterlow mural can be found in the Mary Seacole Hall dining room.

Savacou

The Family

Sculpture: On the Ring Road, in front of the Medical Research Council Laboratories, is an aluminum representation of *Savacou* (mounted in 1965) – a derivation of the Carib word "Sawaku", a mythical Carib Indian god of thunder and strong winds, who became a bird and later a star. Across the Ring Road is the 2003 statue of UWI founding father Sir Philip Sherlock by artist Valerie Bloomfield.

Near the entrance to the Social Science Lecture Theatre is a group of sculptures titled *The Family*, done in 1967, in cement fondu, by Jamaican sculptor Christopher Gonzalez.

In the quadrangle between the original Arts lecture theatres and the Arts administrative block, there are two pieces of sculpture. One is Basil Watson's 10-foot-high stainless steel sculpture *Heaven and Earth*, an abstraction of the human figure which also suggests a musical instrument. Donated to the University by the Jamaica Mutual Life Assurance Society, the purity of the sculpture's stainless steel structure reflects the interrelationship of physical and metaphysical worlds. Nearby, a wall-mounted metal sculpture, *Dancing Lady* by Denise Forbes, depicts a woman, her arms thrown wide in Carnival abandon.

Art Collection: The UWI's art collection, was catalogued and a travelling exhibition prepared as part of the University's fiftieth anniversary in 1998. While the collection is not on permanent exhibition, one section, the A.D. Scott Collection, is housed in the Main Library.

Geology Museum: The Department of Geology, housed in a building named for Sir Henry de la Beche who carried out the first systematic geological mapping of Jamaica, is home to a Geology Museum. This repository for collections, rare specimens and documents includes some 10,000 catalogued specimens from around the world. It is the largest single collection of rocks, minerals and fossils in the English-speaking Caribbean.

Geology Department Obelisk: In front of the department is an obelisk presented by the Geological Society of Jamaica in 1982, to commemorate 21 years of teaching geology at the UWI. Made entirely of local rock, its height is proportional to geologic time, while its base represents the age of the oldest dated rocks in Jamaica – about 120 million years. The top is a pyramid made of aluminum, representing bauxite, Jamaica's main mineral resource.

James W. Lee Collection: An important collection of artefacts and information on the Taino presence in Jamaica, assembled by James Lee, was presented to the University in 2000. It is presently housed in the Archaeology Lab, located inside the bookkeeper's cottage – a relic of the old Mona Estate, behind the UWI Chapel.

UWI Archives: The UWI Archives and Records Management Programme has a mandate to oversee the handling of University records. As such it has in keeping a range of artefacts including the Charter of the UWI, and a collection of stamps designed and produced to raise funds for the University.

UWI Library: In addition to its collection of texts, the University Library's West Indies Collection has in keeping a range of historic photographs, maps, manuscripts and artefacts. These include a piece of the rock of Gibraltar presented to the UWI in commemoration of the Gibraltar Camp era, when more than 1,500 Gibraltarians found refuge from the war in Europe, on the site where the University now stands.

A gift from the people of Gibraltar

Heaven and Earth

Sir Philip Sherlock

The Dancing Lady

The Geology Obelisk

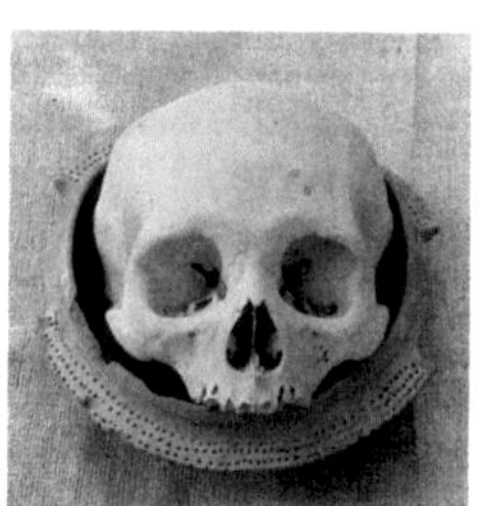

Item in the Lee Collection at the Archaeology Lab

FOR FURTHER READING

This book further develops a chapter on campus history within an MA Heritage Studies research paper, "Heritage and Development at the UWI Mona Campus", Suzanne Francis Brown (UWI, 2001). No footnoting or exhaustive bibliography is provided; however, readers who wish to further explore the subject may find the following references helpful.

Landscape/Geology

Donovan, Stephen K., and Trevor A. Jackson. "Field Guide to the Geology of the University of the West Indies Campus, Mona". *Caribbean Journal of Earth Science* 34 (2000).

Mona Campus History

Afroz, Sultana. "The University of the West Indies – The Mona Campus: A Treasure House of Heritage Monuments, 1998". Unpublished paper filed under Mona Estates, West Indies Collection, UWI Main Library. (A videotaped documentary produced and directed by Dr Afroz, based on the paper, is also on file at the West Indies Collection.)

Edwards, Thera H. "A Floral History of the Mona Campus, UWI". Project in partial fulfilment of a BSc Environmental Science, UWI, 1993. (This report, with a map of historical features on the campus from a 1992 report of the same name, and overlays relating to various historical periods, provides a botano-historical perspective. A copy is on file at the UWI Archive.)

Government of Jamaica. Survey Department. Maps held include an 1888 cadastral map of Jamaica, a 1915 map of Jamaica, and a 1954 photogrammetric survey made from air photographs.

Higman, Barry, et al. "Report to the Principal of the ad hoc Committee on the Preservation and Development of the Historic Features of the Mona Campus". UWI, Mona, 1992. UWI Archive and Records Management Programme.

Morrissey, Mike. *Campus Trails*. Kingston, Jamaica: Department of Education, UWI, 1987. (This booklet is available in the Documentation Centre of the Department of Education, UWI.)

Newspaper records, especially those from the Gleaner Company of Jamaica.

West Indies Collection, UWI. Files relevant to this subject include microfilm records for the sugar estate period, a collection of photographs by Amador Packer, and UWI Historical and Architectural files including illustrations of early designs for the UCWI campus and University Hospital of the West Indies UWI Main Library.

Sugar Estate Period

Chancery Court papers known as "Master Brougham's Exhibits" – referenced in Ken Ingram's *Sources of Jamaican History, 1655–1838* include a 1797 manuscript relating to the Bond Estate, which details the Mona Estate sugar works buildings at the time. Public Record Office, London, UK.

Claypole, W.A. "The Settlement of the Liguanea Plain between 1655 and 1673". *Jamaica Historical Review* 10 (1973).

Cousins, Winifred M. "Freedom in Jamaica". Manuscript adapted from a PhD thesis accepted by the University of London, *c.*1920s. West Indies Collection, UWI Main Library.

duQuesnay, F.J. "Philip Pinnock". *Jamaica Historical Society Bulletin*, no. 4 (1953).

Hakewill, James. *Picturesque Tour of the Island of Jamaica*. London, 1825.

Higman, B.W. *Jamaica Surveyed: Plantation Maps and Plans of the Eighteenth and Nineteenth Centuries.* Kingston, Jamaica: Institute of Jamaica Publications, 1988.

Lewis, C.B. "Some Notes on the Mona Estate". *Jamaica Historical Society Bulletin,* no. 1 (1952).

Long, Edward. *History of Jamaica.* Volumes 2 and 3. London, 1774.

National Library of Jamaica. Survey maps: Mona, Papine and Hope Estates, St Andrew, Jamaica.

University of the West Indies Mona Campus: An Historic Guide. Kingston, Jamaica: Lithographed by the UWI School of Printing, n.d. (This look at the sugar estate period, focusing mainly on the Mona Estate, was written in the late 1960s by Professor David Buisseret, then a lecturer at UWI Mona.)

Yates, Geoffrey S. "A Note on the Origins of the Names Papine and Mona". *Jamaica Historical Society Bulletin,* no. 11 (1955).

Aqueduct/Water Commission Period

Kirkpatrick, W. *A Short History of Over One Hundred Years of the Public Water Supply in the Kingston and Liguanea Area, 1849–1961.* Kingston, Jamaica: The Water Commission (Corporate Area), 1961.

Gibraltar Camp Period

"A Caribbean Jerusalem". BBC Radio 4, 2001.

Cooper, Diana. "A Place in the Sun: The Gibraltar Jewish Refugee Camp". Audio-taped lecture, UWI, Mona, April 2001. UWI Library of the Spoken Word.

Feeney, Fr. William. "Gibraltar Camp". Article printed in the *Gleaner,* 1989. (Copy lodged at the Catholic Chancery, Kingston, Jamaica.)

Finlayson, T.J. *The Fortress Came First.* 3rd ed. Gibraltar: Gibraltar Books, 2000.

Public Record Office. Various Colonial Office, Foreign Office and War Office papers. London, UK. (Some of these papers are also on file at the Jamaica Government Archive in Spanish Town, Jamaica.)

Stanton, M. *Escape from the Inferno of Europe.* London: M. Stanton, 1996.

UCWI/UWI Period

Fraser, Henry, ed. *UWI: A Photographic Journey.* Photographs by Ken Richards and Owen Minott. Kingston, Jamaica: Ian Randle Publishers, 1998.

Hall, Douglas. *The University of the West Indies: A Quinquagenary Calendar, 1948–1998.* Kingston, Jamaica: The Press, University of the West Indies, 1998.

National Library of Jamaica. Historical Notes file.

Norman & Dawbarn. "University College and Medical School of the West Indies: Confidential Report on Sketch Scheme". Norman & Dawbarn, Architects and Consulting Engineers. Bound volumes. London, 1947. UWI Archive.

———. "Chapel for the University College of the West Indies". Norman & Dawbarn, Architects and Consulting Engineers. Bound volumes. London, 1947. UWI Archive.

Sherlock, Philip, and Rex Nettleford. *The University of the West Indies: A Caribbean Response to the Challenge of Change.* London: Macmillan Caribbean, 1990.

UCWI. Archival documents: Minutes, UCWI Provisional Council 1947–1949; UCWI Councils, 1950–; UCWI and UWI Mona Principals' Reports; UWI Calendars; boxed records. UWI Archive.

INDEX